I0799511

Francesca Torzo Building Correctly

ACCATTONE
Architecture Curating Practice
Verlag Der Buchhandlung Walther und Franz König

The text that follows is a revised and expanded version of the lecture that Francesca Torzo gave on 12 May 2022 at the Barcelona Pavilion on the occasion of the Mies van der Rohe Awards 2022. Its title is taken from Pier Luigi Nervi's book *Costruire correttamente* (Milan: Hoepli, 1955).

During a Q&A session, Elizabeth Hatz and Ellis Woodman were invited to join the author and the editors for a brief discussion of the material presented. The projects discussed by Torzo are illustrated with a selection of documents issued by her studio in Genova.

Projects discussed

Building Correctly

a lecture by Francesca Torzo

Ladies and gentlemen,
it is a beautiful day to honour the practice of architecture.

By sharing diverse experiences, we convey a sense of trust, both in our profession and in our society. It is an endeavour towards a better understanding of the practice and its meaning and, consequently, a process in movement which can neither claim the status of a crystallized statement nor indulge in certainties.

In my experience, academic research, design practice, and collaboration between builders and engineers challenge each other with a view to reflect on the human spirit; hence, they have the potential to build a public discourse. With this talk I propose to look backwards and forwards, driven by a curiosity for understanding our way of living and for reflecting on a sense of history. I hope to offer one viewpoint among many in an attempt to find words to share a few questions about the very delicate phenomenon that is architecture.

I will not present works in detail, but will rather accompany the story with references to a handful of projects, some built, others still in development.

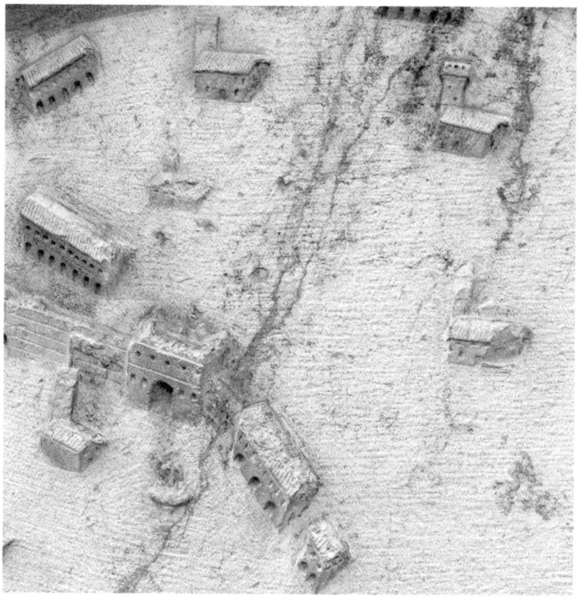

I. Continuity

Santa Maria del
Giglio, Venezia, 2021

Building is one of the oldest human activities, always alive, in transformation. I would say always 'new', as it expresses the limits and possibilities of succeeding societies.

Humans settled and formed their first villages around 11,000 years ago as small clusters of homes dispersed on the hills around the Syrian desert and on the mountains of Anatolia and Iran. Interestingly, they did not settle in the lowlands where, one would imagine, better conditions for cultivation might be available. Instead, they settled on the altitudes, where the mountains offered wild grasses and an abundance of water, which enabled the farming of sheep and goats, pigs and cattle.

1. Fernand Braudel, *La Méditerranée. L'espace et l'histoire* (Paris: Flammarion, 1986).

As French historian Fernand Braudel has observed,[1] the transformation from a nomadic society to a sedentary one – the 'Neolithic Revolution' referenced by historians as the beginning of organized society – was not a single historical event, but rather a slow movement of adjustments, where new social behaviours wove into existing ones.

Some millennia after these first collective settlements around the farming sources up on the Taurus and Zagros mountains bordering the Fertile Crescent, the construction of the first cities began in the neighbouring Mesopotamian lowlands in response to an increase in population and the emergence of different needs. Here, in-between rivers, there were conditions for exchange of goods and the movement of people.

Cities were born in the mazing of roads of land and water.

Z33, painted gips site model, 2012, photo by Philip Lüschen

The roads we walk today, the squares we cross, the houses we inhabit recount thousands of years of geology. They recount the clashes of the tectonic plates of Africa and Europe, the depositing of volcanic ash, and the ebb and flow of waters. They tell how humans settled in various landscapes and how, over centuries, societies consolidated, or altered, parts of them.

Prior to the early twentieth century, the transformation of European cities, to which I can more easily refer, rarely contradicted the initial settlement decisions; they rather confirmed the pre-existing urban and architectural structures, building and growing on them.
Building serves and reveals life.

In the northern lowlands on the border between Belgium and the Netherlands, the city of Hasselt was founded in the seventh century by consolidating the soft soil shaped by the river Demer. The medieval urban skeleton is perceptible in the meandering streets we walk along today and in the burghal clearances of the Begijnhof and the squares.
Here, the citizens have protected the integrity of the beguinage since its construction. Starting in the thirteenth century, it developed over the course of 500 years as an insular architectural complex of houses stitched around a garden and a church.

Z33, painted gips site model, 2012, photos by Philip Lüschen

The beguinage developed as a city within the city, run by women on the borders of society – orphans, widows, rejects – whose exchange of services legitimized their existence. Over time, citizens built on structures of different scope: a building devoted to production in the case of a gin factory and to social representation in that of the museum built in 1958 by engineer Gustaaf Daniëls.

All of these buildings not only preserved the continuity of the built border around the garden, but also adopted the urban *portamento* – an Italian word that addresses the attitude as a manner of gestures assumed in relation to a specific personality or quality – of the beguines' houses, which present almost blind walls towards the street and a filigree of openings towards the interior garden.

The extension of Z33 House for Contemporary Art also observes this non-authorial wisdom of time past, in continuity with the urban *portamento* of all of these buildings from different epochs.

Coloured pencil
drawings, 2020

At the front, a solid continuous brick wall, 60 m long and 11 m high, faces Bonnenfantenstraat. The only three openings are niches of shade, embroidered by plants and not dissimilar to Hasselt's historic passages and urban vestibules, which soften the threshold between the public sphere of the street and the privacy of the courtyards. They act as a breath in the city.

At the back, a dense score of windows facing the garden takes on the rhythm of the façades of the beguines' houses and Daniëls museum. And yet the architectural language differs from the existing buildings.

The expression 'non-authorial wisdom' refers to the reconfirmation of an identity that lies beyond any particular architectural language. Our purpose is not the reproduction so much as the revelation of those qualities that people have found worthy of preservation through the centuries.

Hasselt's citizens safeguarded the border of the beguinage, even as they set about burying rivers, demolishing buildings and erecting new ones. Similarly, in Lucca we find medieval houses built on the foundations of the long demolished Roman amphitheatre. Behind Baron Haussmann's modern *boulevards*, fragments of an older Paris remain. While the bricks and stones of European cities are the product of centuries of evolution, they also testify to the continued significance of deep and enduring urban structures.

Undoubtedly, such urban and anthropic 'substructures' are often rooted in economic necessities – in other words, in the careful management of available resources. And yet the endurance of spaces within the layered body of the built fabric seems to express the innate need of people to belong to lengths of time longer than any individual human life span and to be part of something bigger than just ourselves.

I am interested in inquiring through observation into what people have consolidated in time, sieving the variables which express customs, fashions and conventions that manifest momentary statuses of the individual and the social.
This body of observations about the natural and anthropic history of a place is the palimpsest of our work, so that buildings may belong to the memories of others.

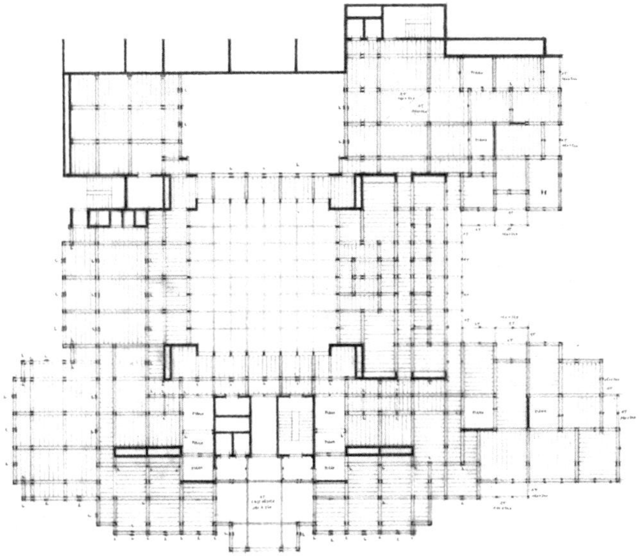

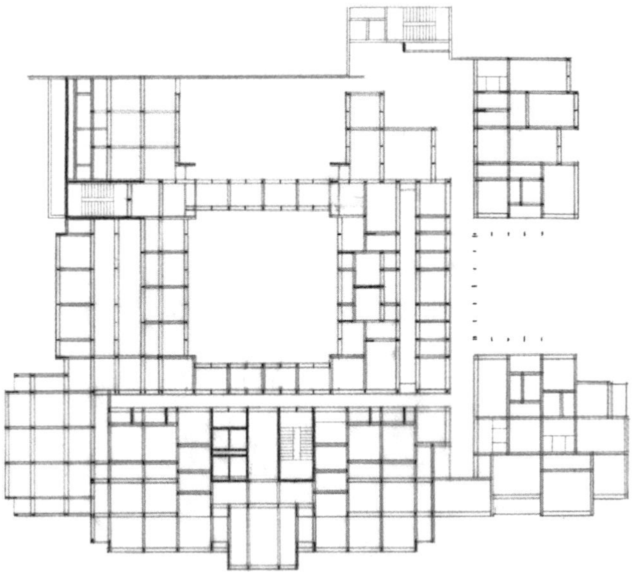

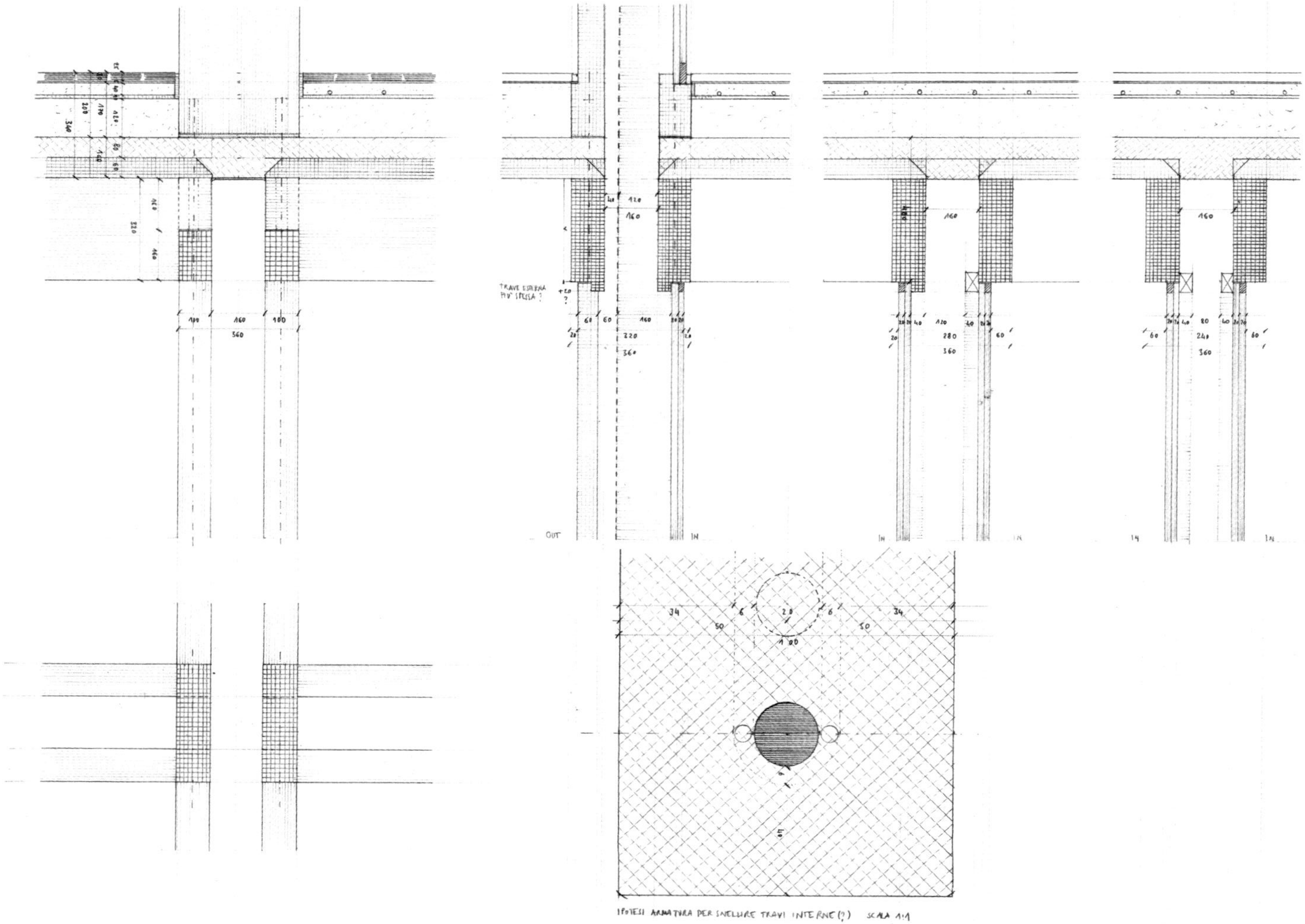
TRAVE ESTERNA PIU' SPESSA ?
OUT
IN
IPOTESI ARMATURA PER SNELLIRE TRAVI INTERNE (?) SCALA 1:1

On the west Riviera Ligure, along the Roman road Via Aurelia, a young doctor from Bergamo bought an expanse of lands that was too poor for cultivation and there, inspired by the civic vision of the Risorgimento, he raised marine hospices for children.

The buildings, whose construction began in 1895, are imbued with the character of city palaces, similar to that *civilization of palaces* evoked by Ennio Poleggi in relation to the sixteenth-century phenomenon of the Genoese palazzi.[2] This was a time when enlightened entrepreneurs built palaces to accommodate and represent their culture, expressing a sense of both pragmatism in the exploitation of the terrain and festivity in the garden scenography. The residential project Villa di Plinio belongs to this culture.

2. Ennio Poleggi, *Genova: Una civiltà di palazzi* (Milan: Silvana, 2002).

Urban character is expressed through the vertical orientation of the façades, which are articulated by a persistent rhythm of pilasters. Terraces, loggias and hanging gardens choreograph an imagined idleness and stage the rite of urban walks.

The columns are thin elements in reinforced concrete, single structures of coupled pillars measuring in plan 110 by 360 mm each. They can be arranged in alternate orientations from floor to floor, allowing different dwelling configurations without compromising the transfer of loads.

Villa di Plinio, marmorino model, 2023

Villa di Plinio, graphite drawing, study of the structure, 2021

Villa di Plinio, graphite drawing, study of the structure, detail, 2021

The mineral expression of the building translates the stone and mortar traditions, but the prefabricated elements are in essence steel structures made of full steel core elements measuring 60 by 60 mm in section covered in concrete, adapting Pier Luigi Nervi's technique of *ferrocemento* to current building regulations, which are much more demanding than those of the twentieth century.[3]

3. Pier Luigi Nervi, Italian patent no. 377969, 'Structural prefabrication technique', Archivio Centrale dello Stato, Fondo Brevetti, Rome, 1939.

This quest for extremely slender dimensions stemmed from the need to achieve the minimum building height – 306 cm floor to floor – and so contain the building's overall volume while preserving the Italian common living height of 270 cm. It follows that the hollow structure of prefabricated beams and pillars provides the infrastructure in which to house all the technical installations.

On the other hand, the freedom of orientation of the structural elements allows for diverse spatial arrangements at each level. The result is a highly diverse dwelling programme, where the apartments are conceived as a continuous space mainly set up on diagonal perspectives as an alternative to the ceremonial enfilades typical of classical rooms.

While the dense programme of almost 10,000 m^2 is arranged across eight floors, we have drawn on the Genoese tradition of invented topographies and garden scenographies to conceal the mass of the building. Villa di Plinio responds to the scale and expression of the villas and palaces that inhabit the coast of Liguria, seeking a dialogue of continuity with the past while eschewing mere formal historicism.

Karl Friedrich Schinkel, reconstruction of Villa di Plinio, 1835

A building is a cultural artefact.

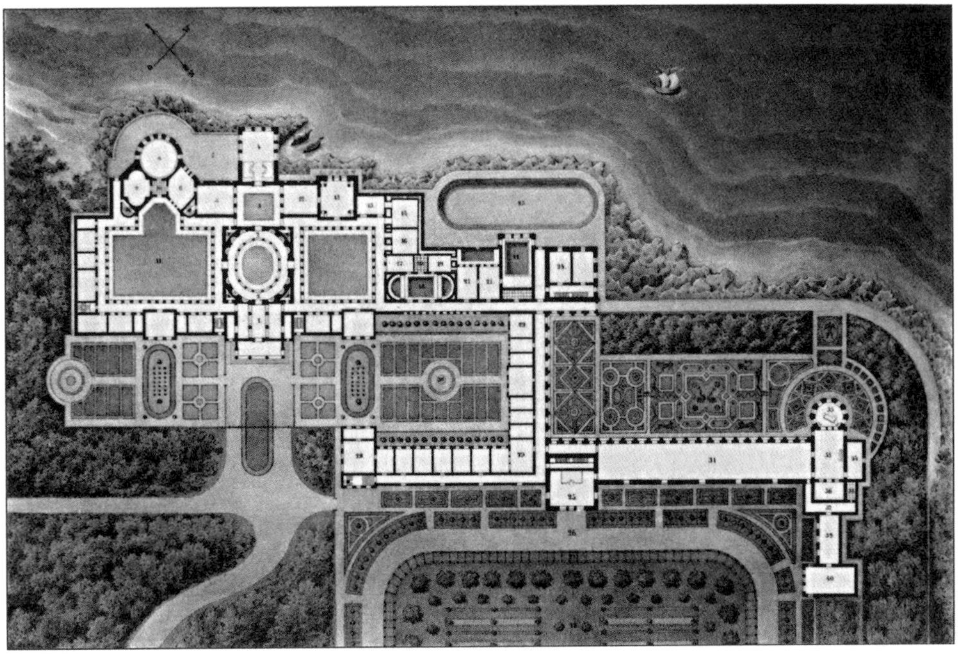

In the 1830s, Karl Friedrich Schinkel produced drawings, enriched in watercolour, that presented imaginative reconstructions of classical Roman villas.
They are drawings of invention, in which the architect imagines the spaces of a Mediterranean Arcadia. He represents Villa di Plinio based on a letter by Pliny the Younger, in which the Roman aristocrat describes to his friend Domizio Apollinare the interior spaces of the villa and the spaces of the gardens as woven in a continuous walk.[4]

4. Pliny The Younger, *Epistulae* V, 6 (100–113), Venice, 1471.

The experience of landscape is orchestrated through the sequencing of rooms of diverse proportions and directions as a double-sided scenography.
The outdoor scene of the garden completes the interior one, enhancing the individuality of each space as a framed tableau. At the same time, the movement from room to room reveals the landscape, giving a sense of orientation, of topography and even governance.

The experience of the landscape is thus achieved through the unpredictable shifting perceptions of different scales – interior and exterior, garden and surrounding territory – and the evocation of past dreams and passions.

Watercolour drawing, study of spatial relations, 2021

We could read palaces and villas as a cultural reflection on the landscape, as in Schinkel's drawings, where the promenades invite us to discover and imagine spaces and narratives. How can we continue someone else's tale and activate these cultural associations, where the interiors and the exteriors elicit each other, offering conditions for the coexistence of both inwardness and exposure?

There appears to be a sense of uncomfort today with the word 'continuity', as if it implied either an authoritarian or disengaged imposition of stasis, withholding individuals and society from growth, freedom and change.
Building is a tool for representing cultural and political powers around which a community may converge and find agreement for a limited period of time. The character of architecture has consequently undergone profound transformations over time. However, it is possible to recognize permanencies in the *cultural structure* of cities, a phrase that seeks to identify that which has survived over the centuries and which constitutes the specificity of any place constructed by humans.

I believe that architects who engage with an idea of 'context' might look beyond the nostalgic figurations of a *genius loci* or the reductivism of the *analogue city*.
In different and contrasting ways, Rossi and Norberg-Schulz's writings represent some of the most refreshing and authentic reactions to the restrictiveness of the Modern Movement's derivations, one addressing collective memory and the other subjective perception as tools to question the meaning of architecture.

But in time, the clarity of their quest has been polarized into quasi-ideological manifestos that lack the richness of the original thoughts.

I wonder whether the idea of 'context' couldn't be loosened from such persistent logics and dare to combine a sense of the individual with a sense of the collective, engaging in those essential relations that people keep alive and share with others, those relations that belong to a wider history and life, *la longue durée.*

Is all that has been not a precondition for being and for inventing our future? [5]

5. Braudel, *La Méditerranée*, cit.

II. Distant dialogues

Casa Due,
Sorano, the stone
walls, 2008

Viterbo, the
historical walls,
2000

A building is a building.
A building is not an object. Nor is it a social or political experiment.

It has weight and size. It remains in place for decades – sometimes for centuries or millennia – and comes to form part of an existing anthropic context, be it an urban or natural landscape.
This 'context' is the layered amalgam of the history of humanity, an infinite intertwining of causes and consequences that change at different velocities, some from day to day, others from year to year, still others from century to century.

Hasselt's historical centre, French palaces, a modernist museum, northern Italian villas. Wandering through streets, alleys, rooms, courtyards, gardens and other rooms, other courtyards, other alleys, people recall familiar images, as familiar as a folk melody or a fable.
In an instant, our minds constantly recompose in unpredictable ways experiences gathered by our senses along with others faraway in time and space and that we keep archived in unknown ways.

An entrance patio, a tree, a fountain.
What do I remember?
What do you remember?

Casa Due, a holiday house in Sorano, between Tuscany and Latium, was previously a shelter for chickens and rabbits: a casual group of small rooms perched on the tuff hill overlooking the river Lente. Sedimentary folds follow one another, as a wilder scenery mottled by chestnuts, wild plums and olive trees. The humble construction stretches in length upon the Orsini Renaissance walls.

From a distance, the village extends along the silhouette of the hill, so that the houses and the topography present a single figure floating over the shades of woods. Inside, the urban maze turns, climbs, descends, seemingly a product of chance and accident. The new building is no exception within this landscape of roof ridges.

Nearby, the historical walls of Viterbo are textured with square tuff blocks, surprisingly laid out in aligned joints, as the stone-cut elements are long and solidly anchored in the amorphous core of the *sack masonry*, several metres thick.

In Casa Due, the narrowness of the plot demanded thin walls to achieve reasonably sized spaces.
We developed an experimental drystone construction to optimize the surface for living while employing stone-cut masonry, similar in character to that of the historical walls and village. Self-supporting trapezoidal tuff blocks are combined in a Janus-faced composition with aligned and staggered joints, and then stabilized by metal minutiae and tensors to compress the mass of stone, resulting in a wall 25 cm thick.

The construction is not historicist, yet it belongs to tradition. The way of living is modern: a continuous space overlooking the vastness of the hills.
It is an arrangement that departs from the vernacular typology, where each room is recognizable as one individual room because of the prevailing size of the surface of the walls in relation to the thresholds, which are proportionally smaller. The sizes of the openings in Casa Due are quite similar to the traditional ones, but proportionally wider in relation to the wall surface, so that an experience of openness prevails.

Is it possible to speak of modernity – or *modernities* – without speaking of tradition?
Aren't modernity and tradition the two sides of one coin, two attitudes of a living culture that do not exist without each other?

Casa Due, 2008, photo by Gion von Albertini

It is commonly understood that modernity refers to a 'present time' frequently in dialectic with – or even opposition to – a 'past time'. Tradition is commonly associated with a 'past time', sometimes invoked as a safe keeper, sometimes opposed as an authoritarian construct.
Nonetheless, if we accept the continuity of human facts, there are no real ruptures, rather a coexistence of endings and beginnings, as Johan Huizinga writes in the preface to *The Waning of the Middle Ages*.[6] We may then recognize a constant coexistence of 'past time' and 'present time' and therefore a coexistence of 'tradition' and 'modernity'.

6. Johan Huizinga, *The Waning of the Middle Ages* (London: Arnold & Co., 1924).

I recognize correspondences among individual and collective memories that layer in a body of unconscious knowledge, which builds up through a process of social sedimentation of the experience of past human activities.
This sense of ahistorical tradition can only reveal itself in the present, when we live.

Yangshuo library pavilion, landscape watercolour, 2019

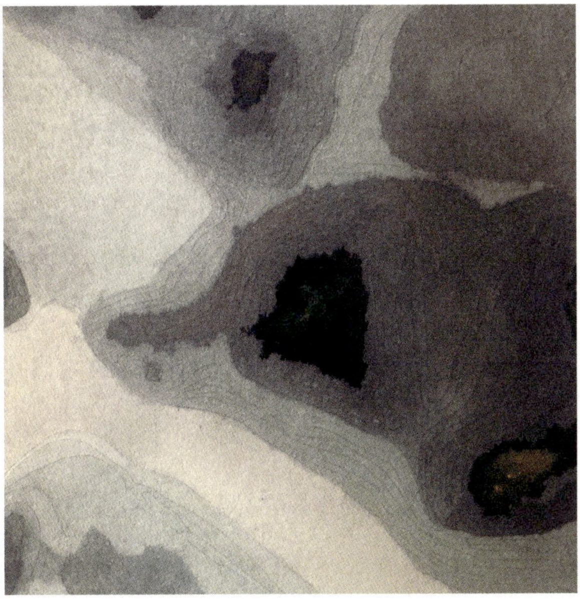

Guilin is a fabled scenery of thousands of majestic peaks of karst limestone. These stones emerged from the collision of India and Asia 40 million years ago and in time weathered, dissolved and were eroded by rain and flowing water. This meandering topography is crossed by rivers, and all the borders between water and land are softened by bamboo woods that reach heights up to 16 m.

It is an ancient landscape where stones, forests and small buildings hold in their names the vastness of an old oral culture. Along the river, people have built small towers that served as landmarks to measure travel distances, as observation points as well as signal stations to guard the river.

The Yangshuo library pavilion is part of this lore.

The dodecagonal building has a core in faded blue pigmented concrete. It offers a robust structure to resist the seasonal floods and provide a base for the bamboo construction developing from the first floor upwards. From the ground-floor *cryptoporticus*, a concrete spiral staircase leads to the small belvedere.

Spaces are articulated through alternating curved surfaces of concrete and knotted bamboo, creating a scenography of varying depth where children may play or find niches to gather and listen to teachers' readings.
These modulations rephrase the alternation of light and shadow that performs at the scale of the landscape in the meandering surfaces of the limestone peaks.

Bamboo is abundant here, yet it is not licensed as a building material although it is widely used for scaffoldings. The construction principle translates the knowledge of basket knotting into a building technique, where bamboo stalks are assembled in elements and then mounted on top of the concrete structure.
The single knot allows a certain degree of adjustment during construction, approximating a myriad of straight segments into curved surfaces that moderate the scale of the building, and lend it a gentler presence.

While sailing down the Yangshuo river, the pavilion may go unnoticed, one among other small artefacts emerging from the bamboo along the banks.

Yangshuo library pavilion, model, 2019

Yangshuo library pavilion, façade model, 2019

In another part of China, in the southern province of Anhui, villages were built at the foot of mountains, establishing a threshold between the steep woods and the fields. They still appear today as long white lime walls lined by dark grey tiles.

Stone carving, Portrait of a courtyard, Han Dynasty, 206 B.C. to 220 A.D.

Bishan dance school, archaeological model, 2019, photo by Julia Nahmani

Huizhou villages were founded by merchants around the fourteenth century as a maze of houses and ancestor halls, an ordered labyrinth of small rooms and small patios, wider rooms and wider patios, all planned according to the principle of water management. Rainwater is guided by vast tiled roofs to the patios, where it is partially stored or directed to the stone channels running along the paving.

The Bishan dance school inhabits an Ancestors' Hall on the border of a Huizhou village. Here, in the 1950s, parts of the courtyard had already been occupied by large, sober storage rooms, while preserving the integrity of the perimeter wall.

An order of arcades is introduced in the 'archaeological site', echoing the pace of varying scales and the chiaroscuro of the historic village. New gardens, new patios, new halls become stages for dancers, or alternatively seating areas for audiences, drawn and connected by a maze of channels and water surfaces.

The pillar plays a crucial role in forging a relationship to the traditional architectures. It sets a rhythm of shadows familiar to the historic village while translating the sequence of interior and exterior spaces perceived in the existing streets, patios and houses into a multiplication of double-sided stages.
The pillars trace porticos that combine the existing halls and courtyards with new halls and new courtyards forming one polycentric scenography.

The construction is the mineral translation of a timber building culture in a region where the condition of having only materials of short length led to mastering the art of wood joinery. Pillars, pulvinus, rafters, beams.

The question arises whether it is legitimate to express a comparable staggering of elements, employing a casting technique with a different tectonic. Casting concrete in the grammar of a staggered construction could in fact be marked as a formal quote or a pantomime of a vernacular figure. I rather wish it to be a suggestion, like the way Marc Bloch addressed the chance of calculating what needs 'precise shadings of verbal tone',[7] exploring what ingredients may let people experience a sense of belonging to a cultural context, even when different from their own.

7. Marc Bloch, *The Historian's Craft* (1949; New York: Knopf, 1953).

In an interview with Channel 4 in July 2020,[8] Werner Herzog reflected on his sense of truth or truthfulness in the narrative construction of films and documentaries and on his curiosity for the universe. He explained how he discovered the world by walking on foot, for miles and miles, in search of authenticity, aware of the fact that although there is no unambiguous truth, a search for the universal is innate in human beings.

8. Werner Herzog,'We Are not Attached to the Real World Enough', interview, Channel 4 News, 2020, https://www.youtube.com/watch?v=jU53E7nB-yo.

Could this desire for the universal unconsciously express the aspiration for a sort of order capable of hosting human ambivalences, as Claude Lévi-Strauss argues?[9] According to him, 'mythical stories are, or seem to be, arbitrary, meaningless, absurd, and yet seem to reappear all over the world'.
Each of us is a kind of crossroads where things happen.

9. Claude Lévi-Strauss, *Myth and Meaning* (London: Routledge, 1978).

I am keen to observe the reality I live in, searching for plausible associations with these fossil fragments – buildings, urban artefacts as much as daily gestures – that bear witness to the history of individuals and societies.[10]
I believe that it is in a rational understanding of the bundles of such relations, more than in isolated relations, that these associations can be put to use and combined so as to produce a meaning that is both historical and ahistorical.

10. Claude Lévi-Strauss, *La pensée sauvage* (Paris: Plon, 1962).

A sequence of remote events that is non revertible is what historians refer to as 'historical'. They recognize sequences of happenings that may provide tools for interpretations of events yet to come, therefore 'ahistorical'.
Myths have this capacity to combine the present and the past as well as the future, relating individual experiences with a sense of the universal without romanticism.
I am more interested in how a building can activate this associative and allusive phenomenon than in taking a position in the moralistic polarizations of true-false, honest-dishonest, right-wrong.

Bishan concrete pillars and rafters play a popular tune.

Belveglio, watercolour of the landscape, 2023

Belveglio, watercolour of the residence, 2023

Gallery MassimoDeCarlo has chosen Monferrato as the site of a cultural foundation. The project questions the identity and function of an art gallery by distancing itself from the metropolitan contexts where their activities have already found a home in distinctive historical architectures.
A number of architects are involved in the scheme: one has been commissioned for the Kunsthalle and overall master plan; we are responsible for the artist residences and ateliers, together with a hall, cafeteria and restaurant.
Our proposal is conceived as a reflection on landscape which views the yet-to-be-built Kunsthalle as a form of castle.

Here the Ligurian Ocean disappeared almost 60 million years ago, becoming a vast saline valley eroded by rivers and glaciers in the course of millions and millions of years and providing an ideal setting for the development of agriculture. Today the landscape appears as a tide of soft long hills that extends as far as the eye can see. Tapestries of vineyards fold over another, dotted by a few medieval castles and a myriad of *casòt*, modest rural buildings used for storage and as a rest area for the peasants, as well as miniature *piloni votivi*, sites of popular devotion that commemorate both Christian saints and pagan myths.

The programme is predominantly housed underground, as the only visible structures at ground level are the three entrance vestibules leading to the artist residences. From a distance they register as three small chapels, their individual silhouettes reading against the vineyard-covered hill and backdropped by the figure of the Kunsthalle.

These vestibules seek a relationship to the iconography of agricultural landscape, as represented in Ambrogio Lorenzetti's frescoes in Siena's Palazzo Pubblico, in Piero della Francesca's Diptych, and in Giorgio Morandi's etchings.
Despite their distinct geographic condition, each painting stages a relation between the land and the artefacts of a kindred character, where human constructions play an individual role in the fields mosaic, each set at a distance from the other in line with the fields governance as it shows, still today, in the Monferrato region.

Descending the staircases, though, one enters a highly internalized realm, quite estranged from the traditional local architecture. The rooms unfold around a patio, unseen from the hill, offering an introverted promenade that provides a reflective distance from the world. An affinity with the interior of a Roman villa is suggested, yet the configuration of spaces is notably freer and unmediated by the traditional articulation of thresholds. The doubling of the triangular shaping of the walls makes their thickness disappear, rendering the perception of the rooms as individual spaces even more ambiguous. Uninterrupted by trabeation, a promenade unfolds as a succession of scenic mortar backdrops in blue-green and ochre tones.

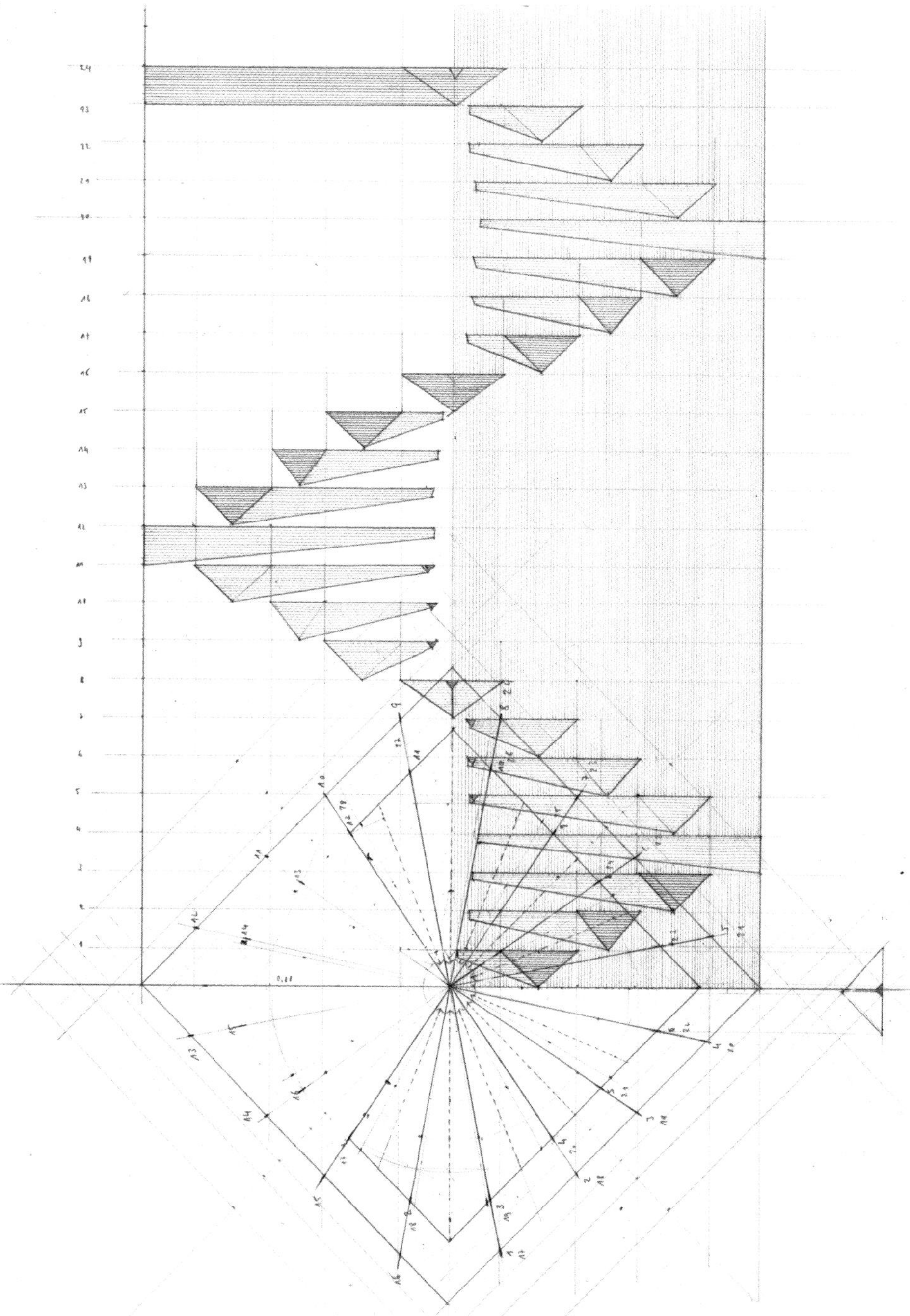

When I speak of 'a castle', 'a chapel' or 'a Roman villa', I rely on a body of precise and open references that all of us somehow share. It is inexplicable as much as the fact that colour-blind people have an understanding of 'red'.[11]

11. Ludwig Wittgenstein, *Remarks on Colour* (1950; Oxford: Blackwell, 1977).

People of different nationalities and backgrounds talk about places using names that we all recognize, enabling a conversation. In addition to this ineffable stratification of shared cultural references, one's own impressions constantly draw from an almost archetypical memory, where the processes of imagination enjoy a higher degree of freedom in combining fragments of experiences of others with one's own.
Sometimes buildings awaken in people memories of other places, even places where they have never been.

The logical system of language is fundamental to our capacity to communicate and share an understanding of things. However, in our efforts to engender a sense of belonging to a place, myth plays the no less essential role of fabulation.
These distant dialogues are mysterious to the individual listener but nonetheless tangible.

In the opening bars of Stravinsky's *The Rite of Spring*, a solo bassoon carries a theme that weaves a Lithuanian folk tune with Carpathian shepherds' songs and melodies from Tibet.

A building is a building.
It reveals dialogues at distances of metres and kilometres, decades and centuries.

Belveglio, graphite drawing, study of the staircase, 2023

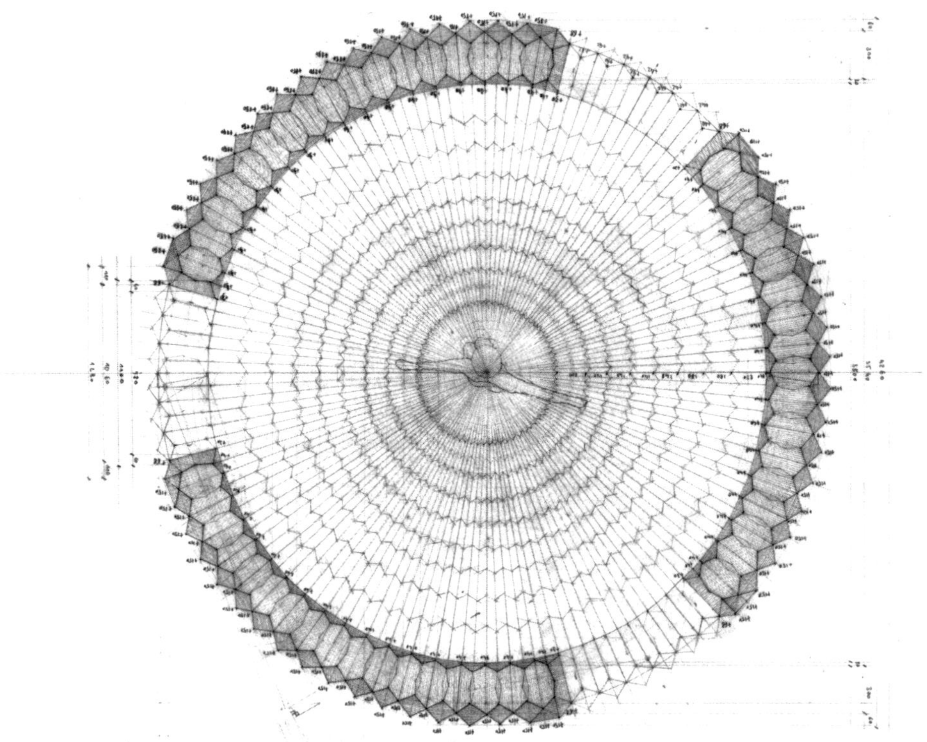

III. Culture and technique

Tenda, graphite
drawing, plan,
2020

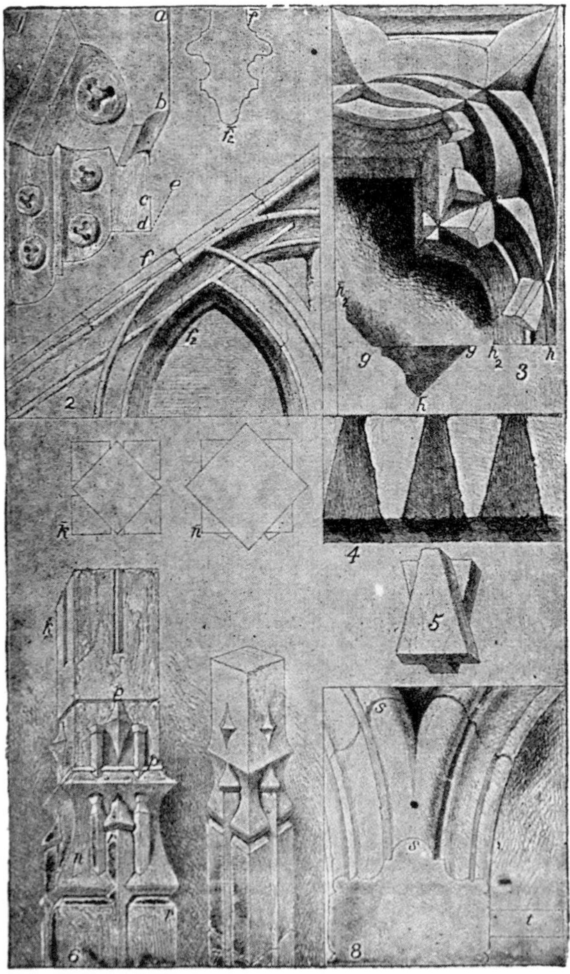

Tenda, graphite drawing, study of the lintel, 2020

John Ruskin, 'The Lamp of Truth', Plate IV, 1849

Drawings note our experiences, observations and memories. A rapid glance may unlock an intuition, a subconscious understanding of a place, a space or a detail. However, until we draw it, until we study its parametric relations and perceptual effects, this intuition remains inaccessible.
Sketches are tools to understand the objects of our curiosity. Geometry then establishes a harmony between the parts and the whole, ordering these relations into a continuous arrangement so that they may correspond to 'the concept in the mind of man', as Leonardo comments on the difficulties of painting life.[12]

12. Leonardo Da Vinci, *Libro di Pittura*, manuscript notes c 1540, first edition, Paris, 1651.

Redrawing, we learn.

John Ruskin redrew the lintel of the side door of Prato Cathedral as a means of illustrating how ordinance comes before necessity, even if the necessity of physical laws is the unavoidable condition.[13]
Stones had to be cut in a way that even if appearing as separate elements – alternately marble and serpentine – they collaborated as one lintel.

13. John Ruskin, 'The Lamp of Truth', in *The Seven Lamps of Architecture* (London: Smith, Elder & Co., 1849).

In Tenda, a small pavilion in *rosato di Verona* stone, the lintel disappears with a similar construction detail.

Invited to contribute with an installation on the theme 'Time in Stone: Beyond the Surface' at the international stone fair in Verona, I wished to propose a space, not a sculpture.[14]
The pavilion is a stereotomic construction of stone blocks, unaided by metal supports or mortar, and hosting a sculpture of a dancing figure.

14. Marmomac, international stone fair accompanied by a series of exhibitions curated by Vincenzo Pavan.

The reflection started with drawing by pencil the stone blocks one by one. The drawing sequence prefigured that of the ultimate construction: the foundation stones and floor, the lintels and threshold columns, and lastly the crowning stone. The drawings gauged the weight of the blocks and the ease with which they could be lifted.
The construction is highly logical but also conceived as an expression of a textile shelter, with the consequence that the lintel fades into folds.

Are necessity and logic sufficient matters for building?

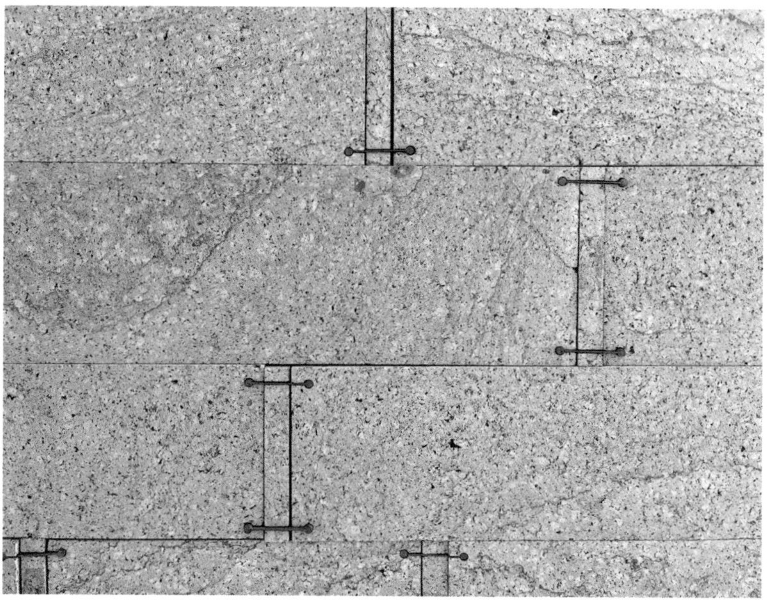

In *Casabella Continuità* 206, published in summer 1955, the editorial by Ernesto Nathan Rogers is titled 'Tradition in Italian Architecture'. This text introduces transcriptions of a public debate held in Milan with Franco Albini, Franca Helg, Marco Zanuso, Giancarlo De Carlo and Gillo Dorfles among the best-known contributors.[15] The discussion is surprising in its candour and centres on a perceived need for reconnection to a figurative architectural tradition, related to both myth and language.

15. 'A Debate on Tradition in Architecture' held on the evening of 14 June 1955 at the headquarters of Movimento di Studi per l'architettura (MSA), an architecture cultural institution founded by Franco Albini in Milano in 1945 and shut down in 1961.

Deeply affected by the tragedies of World War II, these citizens searched for their identity by confronting the present reality – in Albini and Helg's words, 'by perfecting the constants and by thoroughly investigating the possibilities of the variables', where the variables represent 'a way of living, producing, existing' and the constants are those customs, ethics and cultural inheritances capable of surviving society's transformations.[16]

16. Interview with Franca Helg by Cesare De Seta, in *Albini Helg, La Rinascente* (Milano: Abitare Segesta, 1982).

If tradition were to be quoted, it would inevitably result in a formal artifice, mute and sterile for people. However, the work of many architects testifies to how this ambivalent relation to a historical sense can have a plurality of meaningful declinations.

I am keen to detect the cultural phonemes of places, where each has its own previous life history to be brought into the new building and in the structure that brings these old and new phonemes into words.

Porte Contarine, Padova, 2000

Trachite, experimental construction model, 2001

The drystone construction of the Archive of Waters – a built archive of thermic machines, historic maps and drawings related to the Brenta river in Padova – started from the question of how to make a stone building economically feasible in the present day. The project aims to reinterpret the technique of antique lead braces – used to hold the stones together – in a way that is meaningful and expressive of the present time.

The building is a simple ensemble of rooms, built with dry shell walls of *trachite zovonite* stone slabs.

The longitudinal slabs, 100 mm thick and varying in width and length, are stabilized by cross slabs connected through brass braces and by the crowning roof elements anchored to the foundations with post-compressed steel tie-rods.
Since it was an experimental construction, its structural behaviour was unknown. Thanks to engineer Jurg Conzett, we arranged a load test at the Hochschule für Technik und Wirtschaft in Chur, which surprisingly revealed the structure to be stronger than reinforced concrete for a height of 11.75 m.

The construction is *tectonic*; in fact, the higher concentration of cross slabs on the lower courses provides the construction with a low barycentre, therefore stability. Nevertheless, the expression of the façade contradicts the familiar image of traditional stone masonry, where the bigger stones are typically laid at the bottom and become smaller as the wall rises.

Trachite, model,
2001

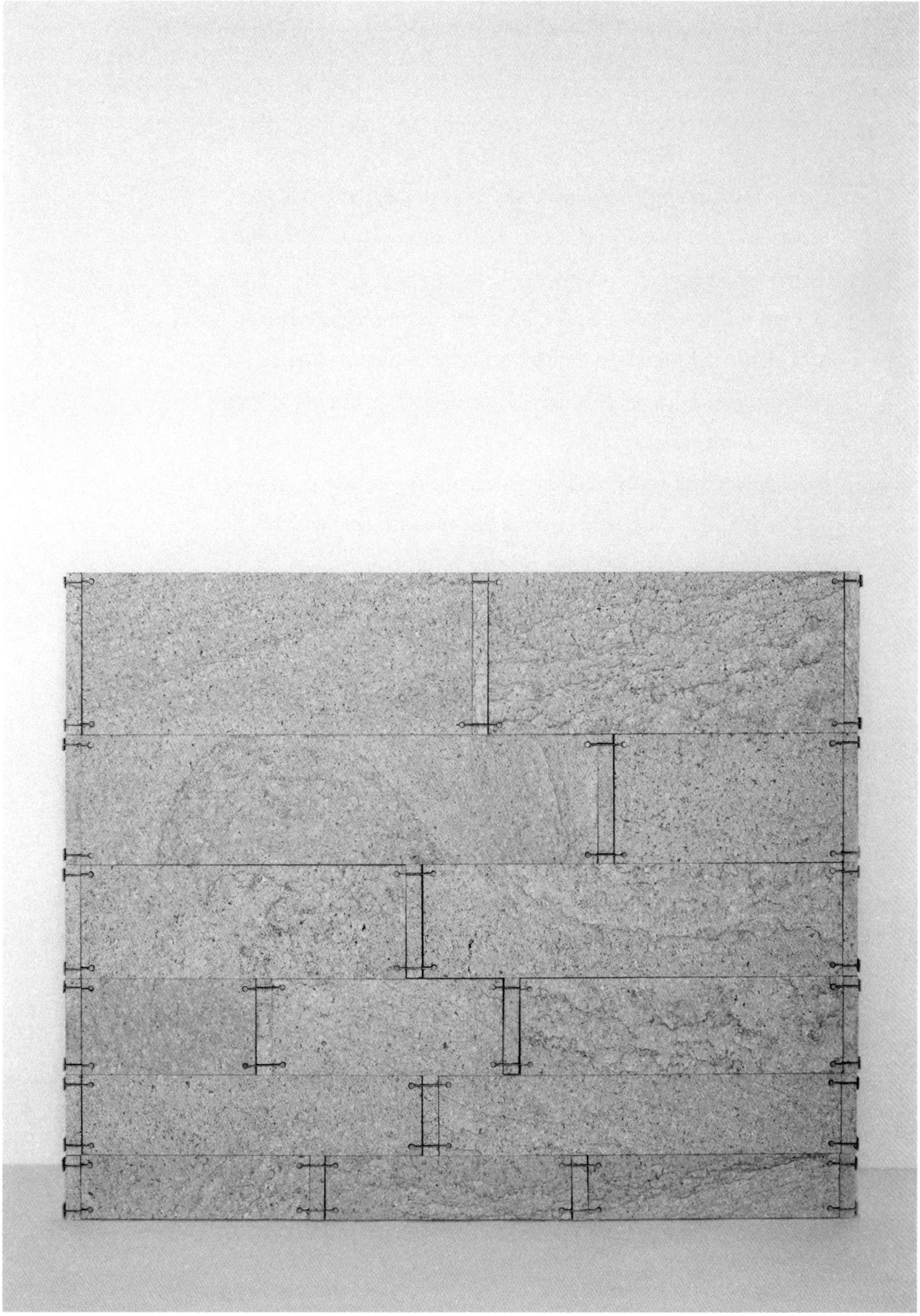

I find the expression 'timeless' misleading. Every act of humanity relates to its time, a play as much as a constitutional act. Buildings depend on their time.

Cultural codes, political agreements, available materials and techniques are always specific to a historical period and cannot be reproduced.
Roman walls – *opus incertum*, *opus reticolatum*, *opus mixtum* – have depths of metres, a depth necessary to anchor myriads of small stones or bricks in a mass of cementitious conglomerate – an unfeasible process today.
And yet we may translate something of the essence of such a structure into an architecture of the present day. We may translate its significance with present means.

In my experience all tools already exist, but they may have been forgotten, or disguised. The tools to build belong to a present living society, but the past offers us ways to think.

Bagni Olmo,
marmorino
model top view,
2023

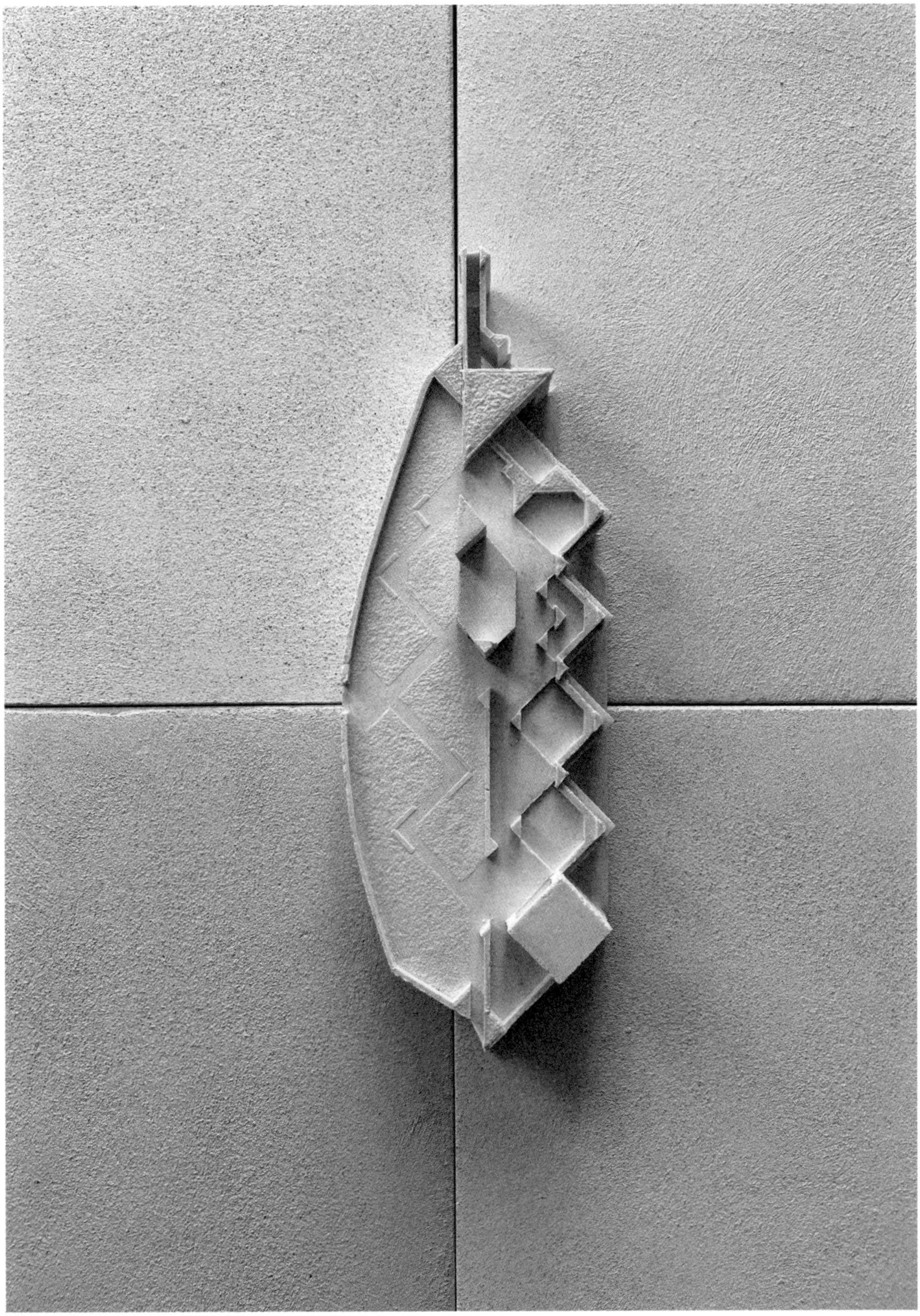

In another part of Italy, on the Ligurian west coast at the foot of the Roman road Via Aurelia, the question of how to reinterpret the material expression of a place has been raised once again. Here the ridges of Punta dell'Olmo and Punta Aspera are bodies of *pietra molare*, a rock born from a submerged sea and shaped by the flow of rivers, resulting in a natural conglomerate similar to a Roman *opus caementicium*.

The restaurant Bagni Olmo stands in this landscape as an archaic mineral building of walls and triangular pillars. It seems to have been carved from the existing stone in a manner evocative of Renaissance grottoes.

To build the restaurant as part of the existing stone seaboard, we started surveying the *pietra molare* aggregates by dimension, lithology and colour. We also searched for stones similar to the natural conglomerate mineral ingredients available in active quarries: metagabbro, serpentinite, jasper, marls and cobbles.

We developed studies on the heights of the successive layers of casting, varying between 200 and 800 mm, in order to take on the scale of the landscape horizontality. We simultaneously tested a number of surface mechanical treatments of the concrete so as to reveal the aggregates in a way that the new walls may evoke the sedimentary geological layers.

The formwork draws the whole plan, so that the building rises as one, layer by layer, with the aim of achieving the perception of a solid concrete construction, where window frames almost disappear.
The sizes of the reinforcement bars have to be strongly differentiated – a primary reinforcement of 25 mm in diameter and a secondary reinforcement of 6 mm in diameter – in order to achieve a thin shell structure able to host technical installations and fulfil stability requirements of construction in aggressive saline environments.

The purpose of all this work is to phrase an architecture as part of a landscape that exists before us, before our parents and grandparents.
To the eyes of the wanderer, it will be a rock, an archaeology or a miniature of conviviality.

I believe that the choice of a material and building method should always be a cultural proposition and that, as architects, we should always be striving towards a technical and cultural maturity rooted in an empathy towards our present reality and that of the past.

Drawing on the image of peripatetic education practised in ancient Greece, the proposal for the new national swimming centre in Tenero was conceived as a set of walkways and pergolas, where the extreme thinness of the structure was crucial to maintaining a sense of exteriority throughout the interior spaces.

The building is a construction of stacked concrete pillars and beams. Precast pillars, measuring 600 by 200 mm, are embedded in the slabs to stabilize the construction against wind and seismic stresses and are connected with a cast-in-place concrete joint to the precast roof beams, measuring 1200 by 200 mm in section for spans of up to 35 m. Beams are connected by steel pins, while the frames of the linear skylights contribute as bracing of the roof beams.
The structural principle is founded on the necessary collaboration of all elements, as their extremely reduced sizes would be insufficient to stabilize the stresses.

This mineral back-lit filigree, daring in its slenderness, aims to transfigure the perception of an interior into a civic agora, a theatre for the people.

Tenero, new national swimming centre, model, 2017, photo by Julia Nahmani

Mindful of Hannah Arendt's distinction between *labour* and *work*,[17] where she proposes the idea that *labour* is merely the process of producing something while *work* is the act of creation of something both memorable and durable, I find myself reflecting on the cultural history of materials and on the ways that they can still be used – albeit within the capacity of the available tools of production – to make buildings capable of embodying collective memories.

17. Hannah Arendt, *The Human Condition* (Chicago: University of Chicago Press, 1958).

Timber and stone, commonly viewed as primitive materials, even in the context of current CNC machines, hold the knowledge that built up on the strokes of axes and the bites of chisels – a culture of whole generations, layered in the various expressions of joining and laying. That legacy forms an appropriate basis for the selection of material and the correct way to work it.
A similar reflection can be extended to concrete, textile, metal, bricks, aware that each material imposes a discipline and carries a cultural narrative.

Z33, façade, 2020, photo by Olmo Peeters

Is a brick old or new?
A brick is a brick.
But what does it mean?

In offering the city of Hasselt a façade appropriate to Z33's public role as a cultural institution, we conceived a wall in the form of an antique textile of diamond-shaped bricks redolent of Roman *opus reticolatum* and of a woven wall.[18]

The long blind wall follows gently the fold of the street. It has a sort of monumentality that fades in the day-to-day gestures, backdrop to walks, chatter and bicycles. Shouldn't monuments be unheard, unnoticed, as Robert Musil warned? [19]
The wall expresses its public presence through silence.

We invested three years to develop, together with consultants, a way to build such a wall under current production constraints, within the legal framework of a public tender and within the small budget set by the client, 1500 euro/m^2.

It began by surveying the historic context: a Munsell chart sampling of the beguinage bricks colour ranges and a *graphite pouncing* survey of each brick. There followed sixty-eight brick colour tests varying the clay mixture and baking temperature, five diamond shape production tests, twenty mortar tests, two façade mock ups, 103 brick types, innumerable meetings and drawings, resulting in an experimental jointless solid façade with 5 mm displacement and a mere 3 mm tolerance.

18. Gottfried Semper, *Der Stil in den technischen und tektonischen Künsten, oder Praktische Aesthetik* (Frankfurt am Main: Verlag für Kunst und Wiss., 1856–60).

19. Robert Musil, 'Monuments', in *Posthumous Papers of a Living Author* (1936; New York: Archipelago, 1988).

The 34,494 bricks were installed by only five men, following a one-by-one m blue pigment grid drawn on the walls as a human-scale reference and tilting each diamond brick on its geometrical centre so as to accommodate unavoidable irregularities.

Naturally, any kind of assignment begins with an assessment of the brief and the budget, as well as the administrative constraints, such as landownership and urban and building regulations. It is precisely in negotiating these constraints, I believe, that architects reveal meaningful relations.

Along with the modern process of life commodification and market globalization, production systems and technical installations agencies have increasingly defined territories of exclusivity, monopolies of building products and a certain degree of communication inaccessibility.

The widespread promotion of the figure of the architect as an 'image director', an aesthetic storyteller often exiled in technical discussions, further limits the opportunities for dialogue between client, builder, architect and engineer.

Building components companies have to fulfil long and economically demanding processes of laboratory certification to comply with regulatory and insurance conditions. This results in limitations to who can withstand the field of experimental research in material production.
On the other hand, craftmanship is often seen as the preserve of alternative-sized structures of production capable of safeguarding individual expression of the design and of the making, walking the edge of exclusivity.

The pressure of delivery schedules and of professional liability often isolates builders from clients and designers, feeding a stance of self-protection which shows reluctancy, if not hostility, towards details or construction systems that do not follow a standard.

Z33, 2019

Ercolano, 2011

These dynamics steer the construction industry towards a diffuse production of generic buildings. However, I believe that investing trust and commitment in starting up the dialogue between disciplines and players in the construction industry can help transform these dynamics.
Experience has shown us that it is possible to challenge the conventional pattern of professional roles and building procedures, which are often the product of comfort zones and are tied to a fear of change.

Bagni Olmo,
graphite drawing,
studies of the
beams and pillar,
detail, 2021

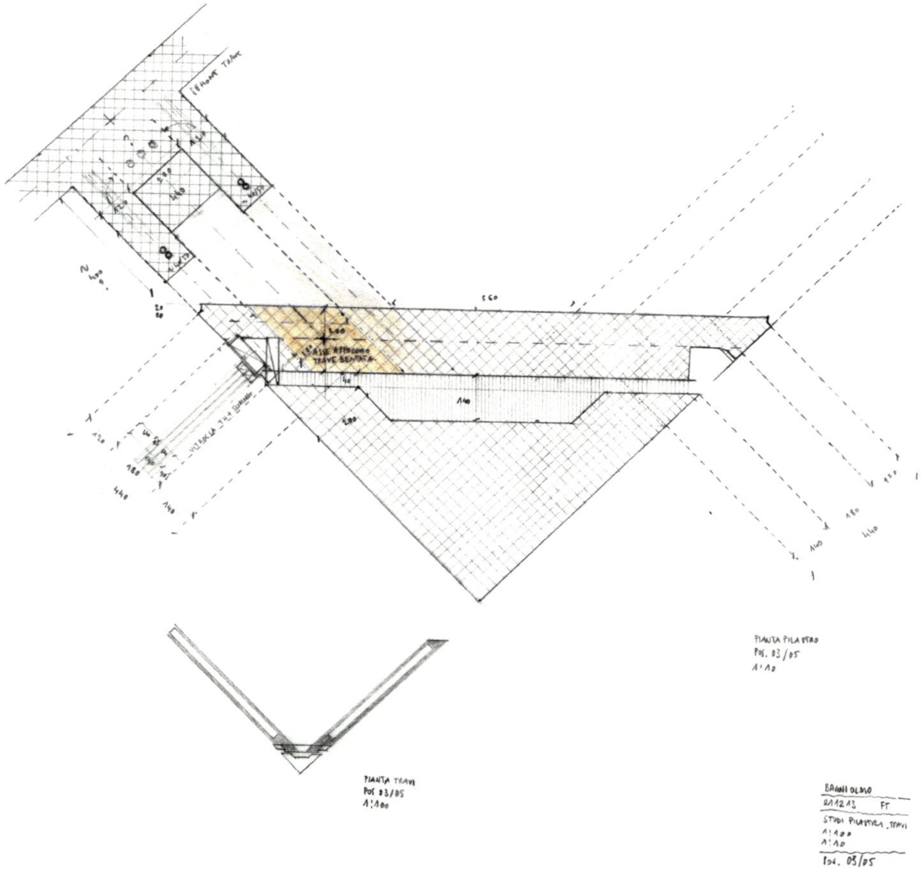

PIANTA PILASTRO
POS. 03/05
1:10
PIANTA TRAVI
POS 03/05
1:100
BAGNI OLMO
21.12.13 FT
STUDI PILASTRI, TRAVI
1:100
1:10
POS. 03/05

A building is the result of the work of many people.

From a very early stage we start an intense production of drawings on very diverse scales, which are often seen as far exceeding the expected quantity and standard level of detail. This work is necessary for us to learn about the building as a body of bone, flesh and veins, where disciplines are invited to participate in a dialogue emancipated from specialistic frameworks.

The collaboration of different knowledges is nothing new in the art of building, but the pace of today's building processes tends to strengthen professional niches.
By making models and tracing drawings we expose our hypotheses to scrutiny.
We work to provide tools to build an agreement based on a recognition of individual stances, but without losing sight of the essence of the spatial narrative.

A mayor of a city may struggle to defend a public political and economic commitment towards a planned building if they are not supported by solid imagery and a reasoned understanding of what they are committing to.
A builder may be uncomfortable with brick masonry for lack of qualified workers, or they may be sceptical towards applying lime by brush because of a lack of experience or due to time constraints.
A municipal officer may be reluctant to take responsibility for interpretating regulations, pressured by the widespread habit of making legal complaints.

From experience I have learned how important it is to listen to the doubts of professional actors and, by understanding the core of the objections, to propose an alternative solution.
I have also learned how important it is to inspire a sense of pride and commitment for the building to come.
When people work with a purpose and a sense of dignity, even difficult tasks become achievable with limited means.

IV. Collective dignity

Ca' d'oro,
Venice, 2022

Van Caeneghem
Blind Asylum,
Ghent, 2019

A building is a building.
A building is in the ownership of people we mostly do not know.

An architectural assignment has inherent characteristics of contingency and specificity. There is a client, whether private or public; there is an architect and a team of engineers; there is a builder with workers and subcontractors. However, these conditions of social and economic specificity exist fleetingly compared to the life spans of the built architecture.
Buildings arise from the singularity of a need, supported by the convergence of economic capacities and ambitions. Nonetheless, while the performance to a specific programme or function fades, stones and bricks, steel and glass show endurance.
These remains of human endeavours are the theatre of people's daily lives and rituals. Moreover, they carry with them impressions and traces of cultural stratifications that, in their interweaving, seem to form the legacy of a collective consciousness.

Buildings are full of echoes, memories, associations. They have been out and about, on people's lips with a name that they could share, in their houses, in the streets, in the fields, for so many centuries. We name a room as others did in the time of the Medici or a few decades ago. Is it the same room?
It is and it is not.
Buildings are stored with meanings, with memories; they are many-sided. Thus, they mean one thing to one person, another thing to another person.
In this apparent disorder there are recurrent themes – or mythemes – that suggest a sort of order which is revealed in a non-linear process of repetition.

A reasoning on mythical structures seems to offer rational tools for observing these ambivalences and paradoxes of human culture.
Sceptical as to any kind of mystical or romantic attitude, I am focused on searching for invariants among transient differences, persuaded that, despite the alienation characteristic of modern societies, people constantly refer to a shared, sedimented memory.

How can we stitch up a language, a grammar, a *portamento* that reflects our lives and culture in spaces?
And how can we combine the past spaces in new orders so that they become part of this vast collective narrative, so that people live them with meaning, so that they create beauty?
That is the question.

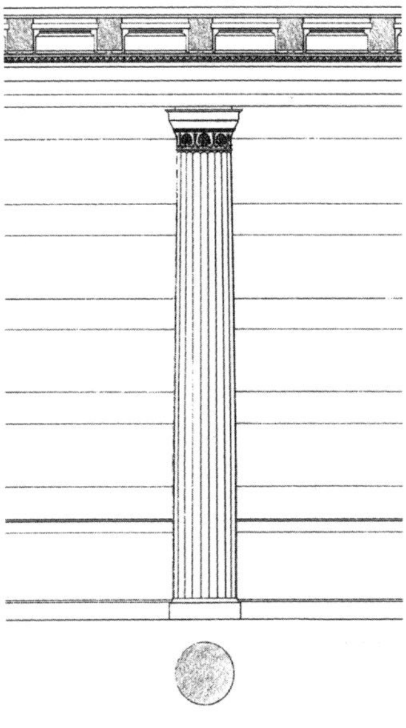

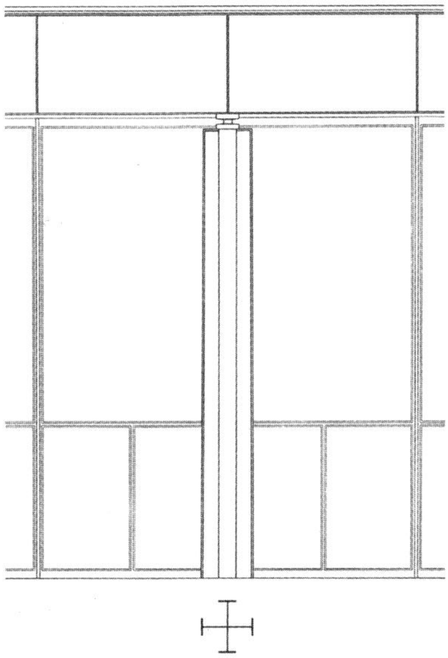

Leon Battista Alberti wrote that the purpose of architecture is to provide beauty as well as to satisfy necessity. For centuries, all arts have had the goal of beauty through the mastery of technique. But strangely, present-day societies often seem to address beauty as something subjective, an individual aesthetic.

Could beauty be readdressed as collective dignity, the decor of citizens?
And how can architects serve this sense of dignity?

Human beings cannot be without a sense of wonder. They need to continually renew a meaningful relation to the facts of their lives, thus finding a dignity of their own.
We architects should assume people's intelligence as much as their vulnerability and recognize their need to reconnect to a shared memory that lives off a combination of present and past.

Aren't the Neue Nationalgalerie and the Altes Museum columns in Berlin 'one' column, one same culture phrased in languages, forms and building techniques a century and more apart? These distant dialogues seem to find substance in the specificity of relations among the parts, in the repetition of these mythemes that people can recognize and relate to. They are fascinating and believable.

The tools of architects are culture and technique.

Karl Friedrich Schinkel, Altes Museum, Berlin, 1825–30

Ludwig Mies van der Rohe, Neue Nationalgalerie, Berlin, 1962–68

'We want to put our feet firmly on the ground, but we want to reach for the clouds with our heads.'
Mies van der Rohe, 1924

Thank you.

Kolbe Museum,
Berlin, 2017

Thorvaldsen
Museum,
Copenhagen,
2015

Documents

Cavalluccio

YEAR 2020 CLIENT Maniera OBJECT bottle opener MATERIAL polished stainless steel SIZE 17.5 × 2 × 2 cm
PRODUCTION Luciano Frascio, Ferremi Leonino

Z33 House for Contemporary Art, Design and Architecture

LOCATION Hasselt, Belgium YEAR [COMPETITION] 08/2011 – 08/2012 [START DESIGN] 09/2012 [BUILDING SITE] 06/2017 – 11/2019 CLIENT Provincie Limburg & Z33 PROGRAMME 3579 m² new construction + 1867 m² renovation Vleugel '58 + 300 m² exterior CONSTRUCTION COSTS € 8,100,000 excl. VAT CONTRACTOR THV Houben Belemco, Kristof Mutert (Houben), Michiel Wielockx (Belemco) STRUCTURAL ENGINEERING ABT België STABILITY ADVISOR Gianfranco Bronzini, Conzett Bronzini Partner ELECTRICAL AND MECHANICAL ENGINEERING Imtech INSTALLATIONS ADVISOR Luca Pietro Gattoni EXPO LIGHT ADVISOR Ben Boving OTHER CONSULTANTS Petersen Tegl, Bekaert, Knauf, Reynaers LANDSCAPE Vera Scaccabarozzi, Lorenzo Rebediani, RSL Rebediani Scaccabarozzi Landscapes SITE SUPERVISION Francesca Torzo LOCAL ADMINISTRATION ABT België TEAM PROJECT LEADER Marco Guerra TEAM Antoine Lebot, Liaohui Guo, Pablo Brenas, Anna Opitz, Riccardo Amarri, Lorenzo Gatta, Előd Zoltan Golicza, Cyril Kamber, Besart Krasniqi, Jovan Minic, Andrea Nardi, Anna Oliva, Costanza Passuello, Alessandro Pecci, Domenico Singha Pedroli, Nicola Torniamenti, Gion Balthasar von Albertini PHOTOS Gion Balthasar von Albertini, Olmo Peeters, Francesca Torzo

Villa di Plinio

LOCATION Celle Ligure, Italy YEAR [START DESIGN] 06/2021 [START BUILDING SITE] 2025 CLIENT Punta dell'Olmo s.p.a. PROGRAMME 3026 m² housing + 2588 m² swimming pool, spa, restaurant and services + 2024 m² underground parking + 1455 m² common gardens and outdoor spaces STRUCTURAL ENGINEERING Fabio Sibaud STABILITY ADVISOR Gianfranco Bronzini, Conzett Bronzini Partner ELECTRICAL AND MECHANICAL ENGINEERING Andrea Muzio LANDSCAPE Vera Scaccabarozzi, Lorenzo Rebediani, RSL Rebediani Scaccabarozzi Landscapes TEAM PROJECT LEADER Leone di Robilant TEAM Isabel Diaz del Castillo, August Kraft Fossmark, Giovanni Rinaldi, Maksym Bal, Nicolò Conti, Massimo Contini, Giacoma Di Vieste, Julia Nahmani, Gabriele Pace, Silvia Ponte, Yian Tian

Larga

YEAR 2020 CLIENT Maniera OBJECT chair MATERIAL walnut, cane SIZE 51 × 63 × 63 cm PRODUCTION Davide Complojer

Casa Due

LOCATION Sorano, Italy YEAR 2004–2010 PROGRAMME 75 m² holiday house + 300 m² garden CONSTRUCTION COSTS € 350,000 incl. interior furniture, excl. VAT STRUCTURAL ENGINEERING Stefano Debiasi CONTRACTOR Maurizio Crociani, Domenico De Feo STRUCTURAL CONSOLIDATION SO.GE.TEC IMPERMEABILIZATION Tecnocolor STONE Marmi Galli METAL CARPENTRY De Rossi, Fratelli Lodoli METAL WINDOWS Fabbri Canton WOOD CEILING Holzbau WOOD FURNITURE Oberrauch PHOTOS Gion Balthasar von Albertini, Francesca Torzo

Pesto

YEAR 2020 CLIENT Maniera OBJECT grinder MATERIAL marble (Verde Guatemala) SIZE 26 × 26 × 5 cm
PRODUCTION Odone marmi

Yangshuo Library Pavilion

LOCATION Yangshuo, Guilin, China YEAR [START DESIGN] 2019 CLIENT Yangshuo landmark tourism development co.
PROGRAMME 180 m² pavilion + landscape walk TEAM Liaohui Guo, Anna Opitz, Shaohan Tang, Yang Tian

Bishan Dance School

LOCATION Bishan, Huangshan, China YEAR [START DESIGN] 2019 CLIENT Huangshan Bishan tourism development co.
PROGRAMME 2000 m² + exterior 3000 m² TEAM Liaohui Guo, Pablo Brenas, Marco Guerra, Antoine Lebot

Chaosmos

LOCATION Palazzo della Triennale, Milano, Italy YEAR 2020 CLIENT Triennale Milano CURATOR Joseph Grima PROGRAMME solo exhibition CONSTRUCTION COSTS € 60,000 incl. furniture, excl. VAT METAL WORKS Luciano Frascio, Ferremi Leonino TEXTILE WORKS Ezio Toccafondi, Meloni & Toccafondi TEXTILES Kvadrat WOOD WORKS Oberrauch LIGHTING Marzorati Impianti VIDEO AND AUDIO Airone service Srl SPECIAL INSTALLATION Edilvago Srl TEAM Marco Guerra, Liaohui Guo, Pablo Brenas, Giacoma Di Vieste, Julia Nahamni, Shaohan Tang, Yang Tian

Massimo De Carlo, artist residencies
LOCATION Belveglio, Italy YEAR 2023 invited competition, winning proposal, ongoing development project
CLIENT Massimo De Carlo PROGRAMME 2701 m² artist residency and public services STRUCTURAL ENGINEERING Gianfranco Bronzini, Conzett Bronzini Partner TEAM PROJECT LEADER August Kraft Fossmark TEAM Leone di Robilant, Giovanni Rinaldi, Maksym Bal, Nicolò Conti, Giacoma Di Vieste, Gabriele Pace, Silvia Ponte, Yang Tian

Dondolo
YEAR 2020 CLIENT Maniera OBJECT swinging garment rack MATERIAL oxidized brass, leather SIZE 90 × 74 × 68 cm
PRODUCTION Luciano Frascio, Ferremi Leonino

Tenda
LOCATION Verona, Italy YEAR 2021 CLIENT Marmomac PROGRAMME 7 m² stone pavilion TEAM Julia Nahmani, Liaohui Guo, Silvia Ponte

Trachite Archive of Waters
LOCATION Padova, Italy YEAR 2000–2001 PROGRAMME 676 m² archive and museum + 20 m² garden STABILITY TUTOR Jurg Conzett with Riet Rageth-Zulauf, HTW Chur STONE QUARRY Trachite Euganea STONE PRODUCTION Valsecchi Marmi, Graniti & Gres METAL CARPENTRY DSG STAMINA LOAD TEST Hochschule für Technik und Wirtshaft Chur

Paolo
YEAR 2020 CLIENT Maniera OBJECT foldable lounge chair MATERIAL oxidized brass, steel, ebony, cotton + linen (Creta Elite) SIZE 66 × 71 × 80 cm PRODUCTION Luciano Frascio, Ferremi Leonino; Ezio Toccafondi, Meloni & Toccafondi

CST
LOCATION Tenero, Ticino, Switzerland YEAR 2017 competition CLIENT UFCL Ufficio federale delle costruzioni e della logistica PROGRAMME 5631 m² national swimming sport centre + 89600 m² outdoor spaces STRUCTURAL ENGINEERING Gianfranco Bronzini, Conzett Bronzini Partner ELECTRICAL AND MECHANICAL ENGINEERING Luca Pietro Gattoni
LANDSCAPE Maurus Schifferli TEAM Riccardo Amarri, Marco Guerra, Antoine Lebot, Andrea Nardi, Alessandro Pecci, Domenico Singha Pedroli

Drago
YEAR 2020 CLIENT Maniera OBJECT throw MATERIAL folded trevira (Kvadrat) SIZE 214 × 125 cm
PRODUCTION Barbagli plisse; Marco Scattaro, Bottero studio

Bagni Olmo
LOCATION Varazze, Italy YEAR [START DESIGN] 08/2021 [START BUILDING SITE] 2025 CLIENT Punta dell'Olmo s.p.a.
PROGRAMME 694 m² restaurant + 186 m² technical spaces + 943 m² exterior + new bridge extension + more than 2 km riverbank naturalization STRUCTURAL ENGINEERING Fabio Sibaud STABILITY ADVISOR Gianfranco Bronzini, Conzett Bronzini Partner ELECTRICAL AND MECHANICAL ENGINEERING Andrea Muzio LANDSCAPE Vera Scaccabarozzi, Lorenzo Rebediani, RSL Rebediani Scaccabarozzi Landscapes TEAM PROJECT LEADER August Kraft Fossmark TEAM Nicolas de Wispelaere, Leone di Robilant, Giovanni Rinaldi, Nicolò Conti, Massimo Contini, Giacoma Di Vieste, Julia Nahmani, Gabriele Pace, Silvia Ponte Yian Tian

Ottomano
YEAR 2020 CLIENT Maniera OBJECT 3-seater MATERIAL walnut, foam, goose feathers, silk velvet (l'Opificio)
SIZE 223 × 107 × 80 cm PRODUCTION Davide Complojer; Ezio Toccafondi, Meloni & Toccafondi

Francesca Torzo architetto, present collaborators
Yannis Barbas, Nicolas de Wispelaere, Isabel Diaz del Castillo, Leone di Robilant, August Kraft Fossmark, Petra Keane, Giovanni Rinaldi

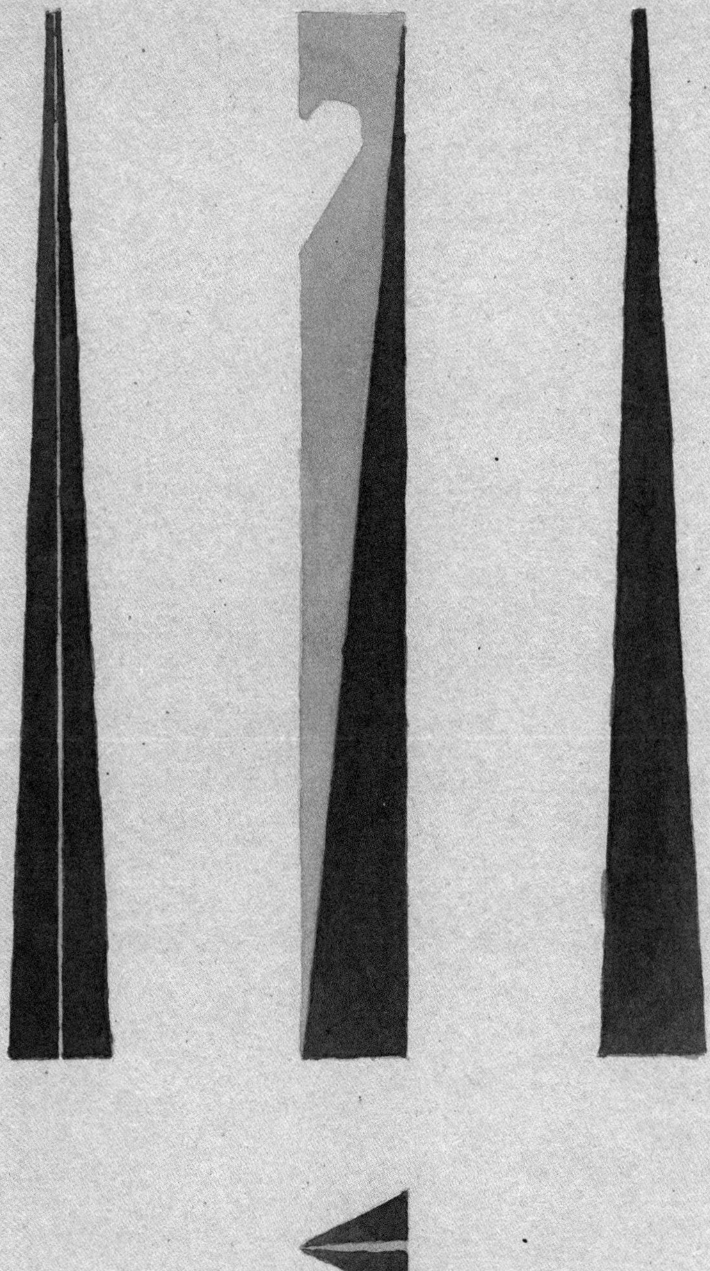

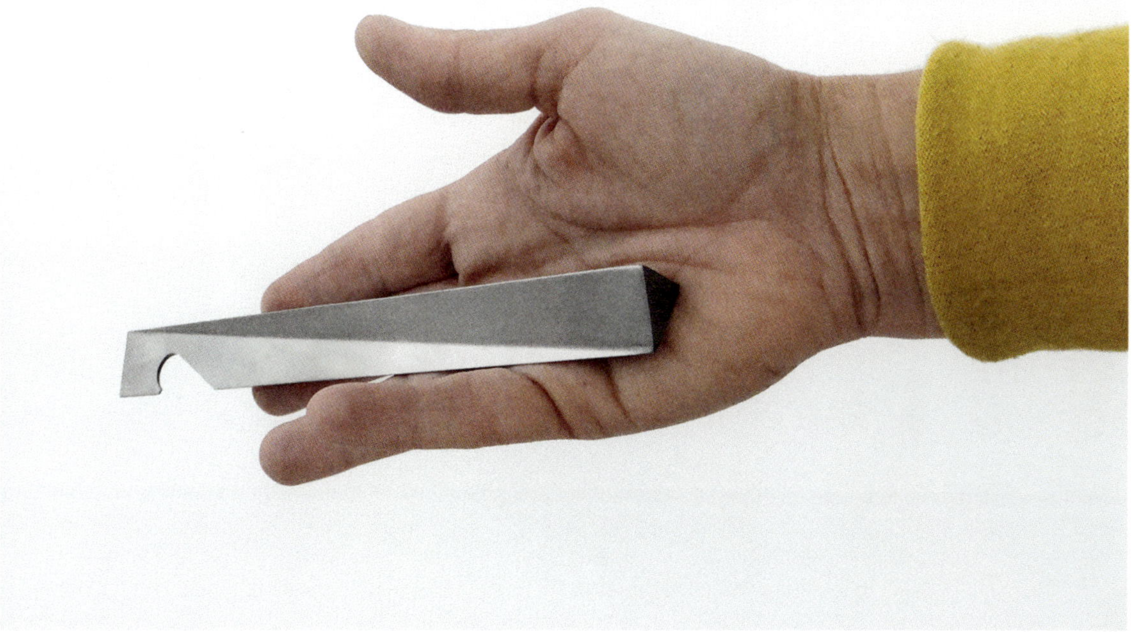

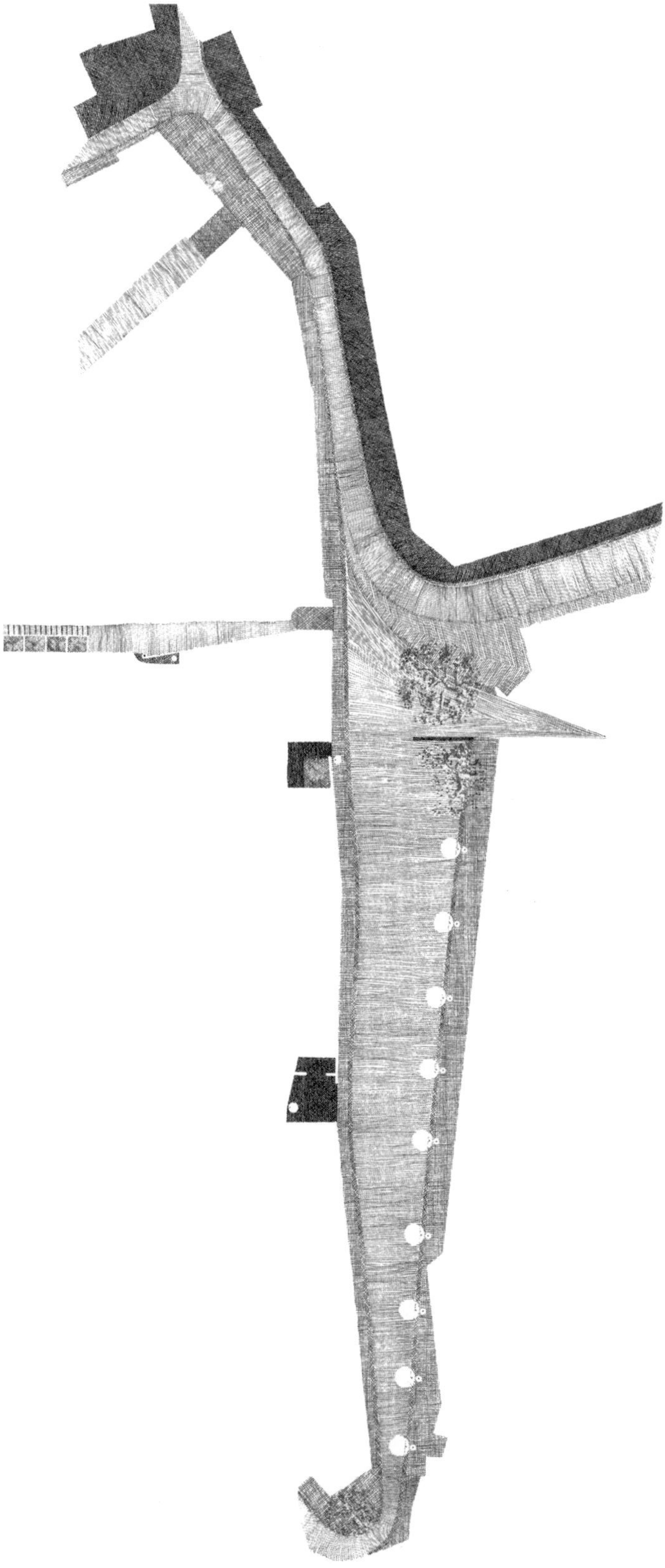

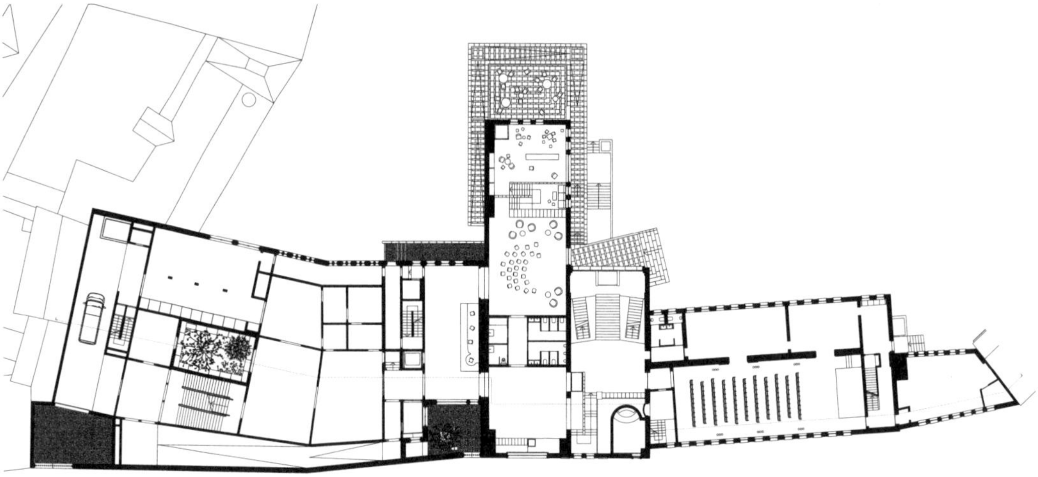

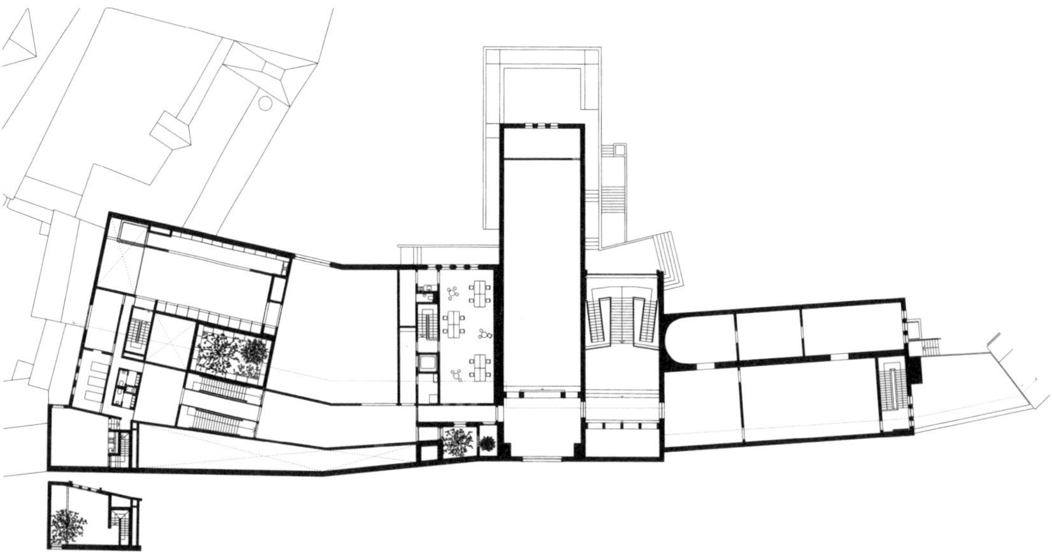

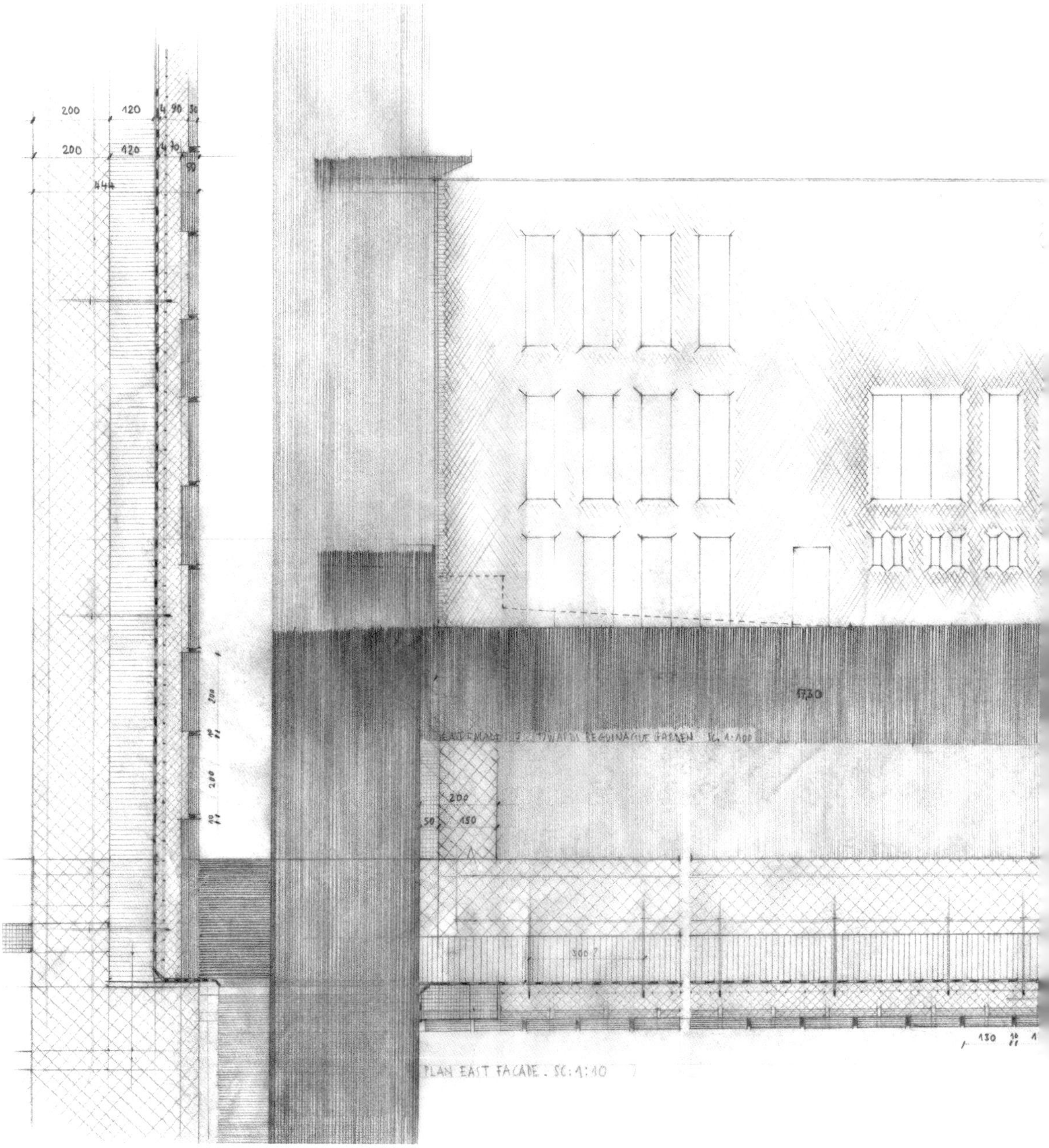
TOWARDS BEGUINAGE GARDEN SC. 1:100
PLAN EAST FACADE . SC: 1:40

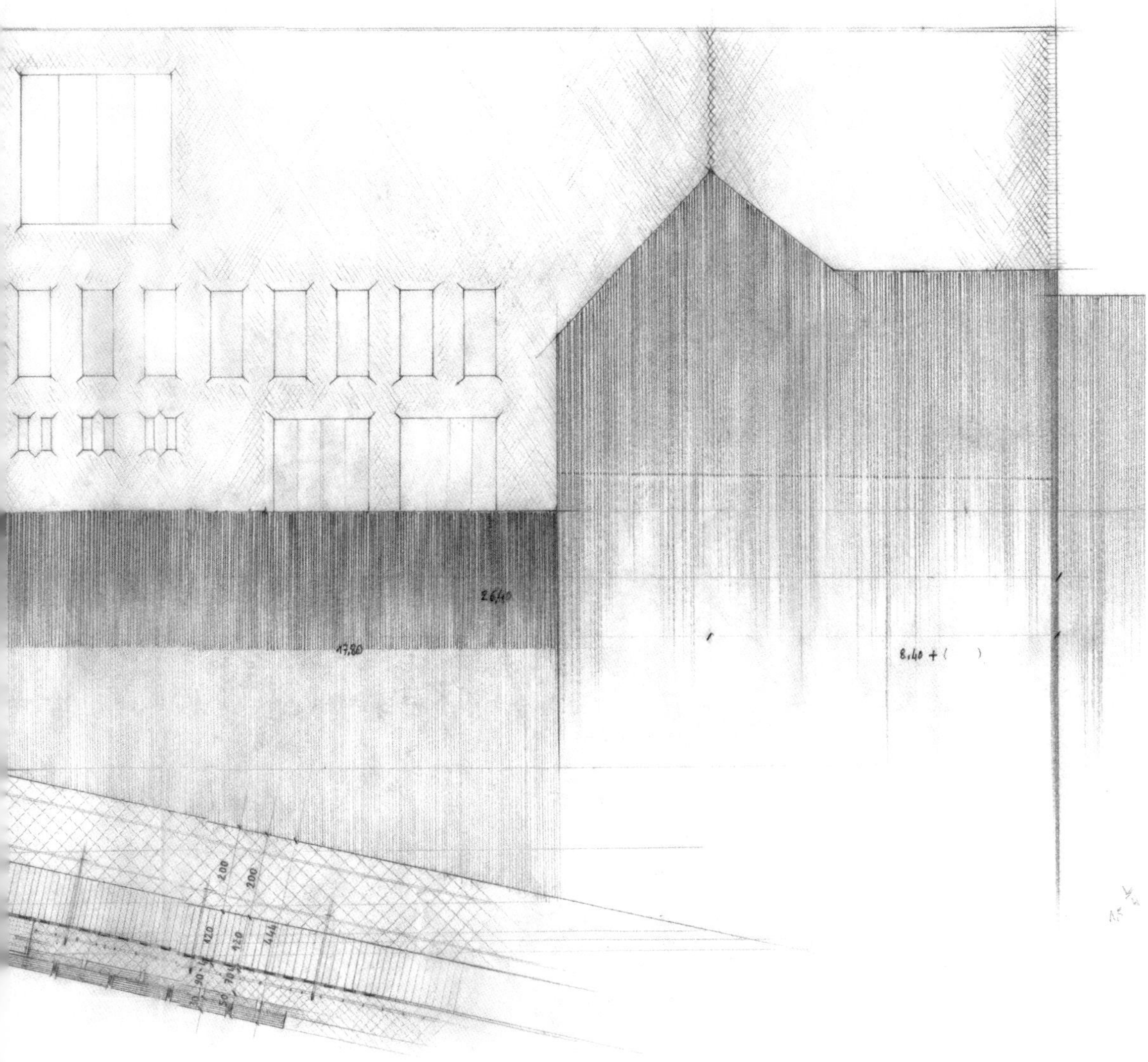
26,40
17,80
8,40 + (   )

Villa di Plinio, housing, Celle Ligure, Italy

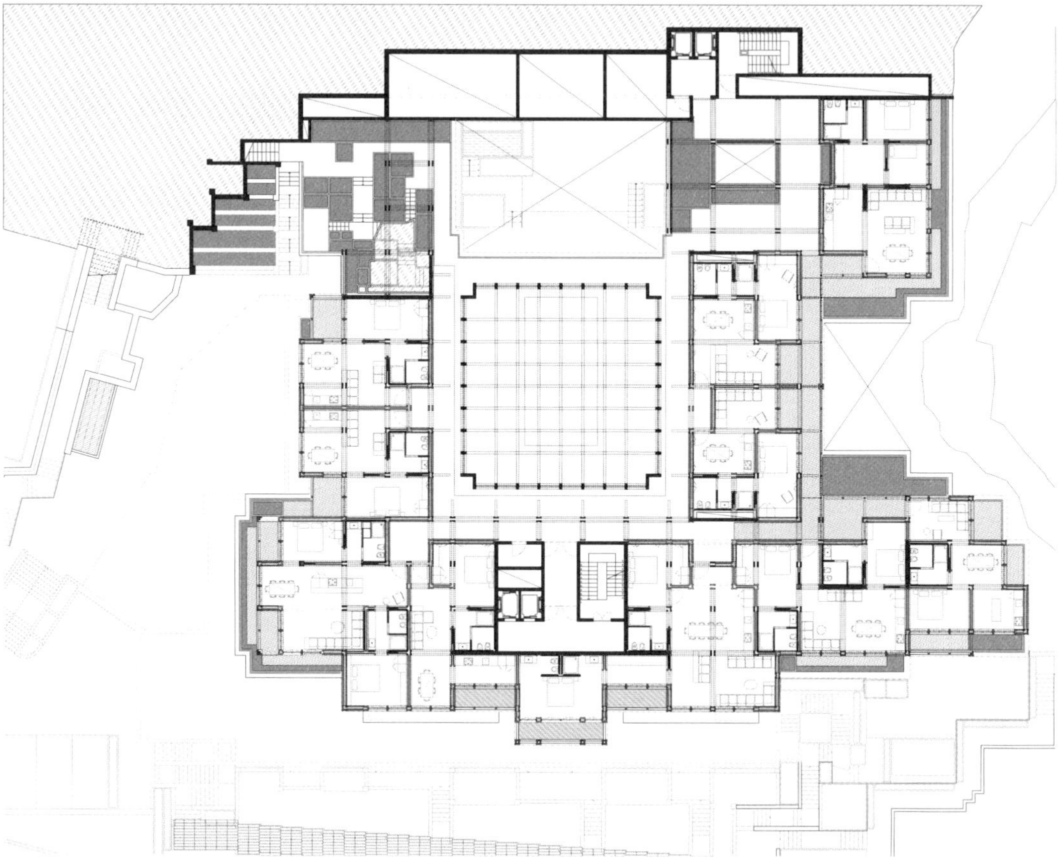

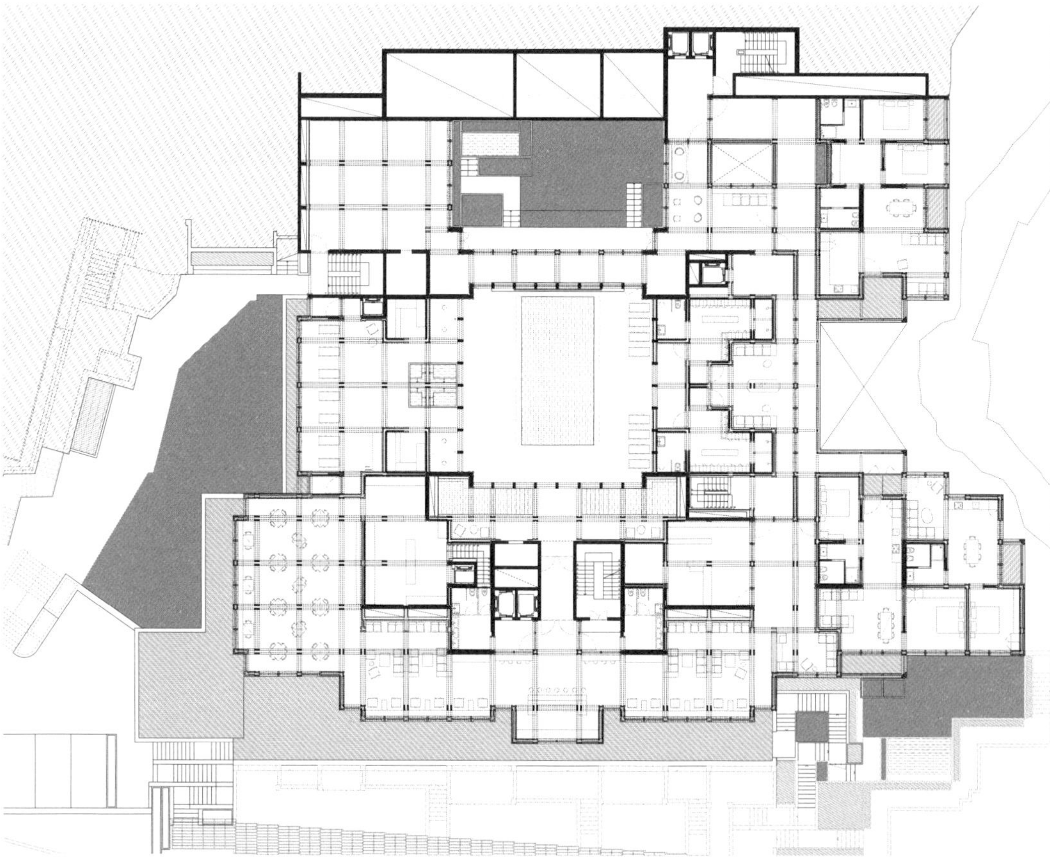

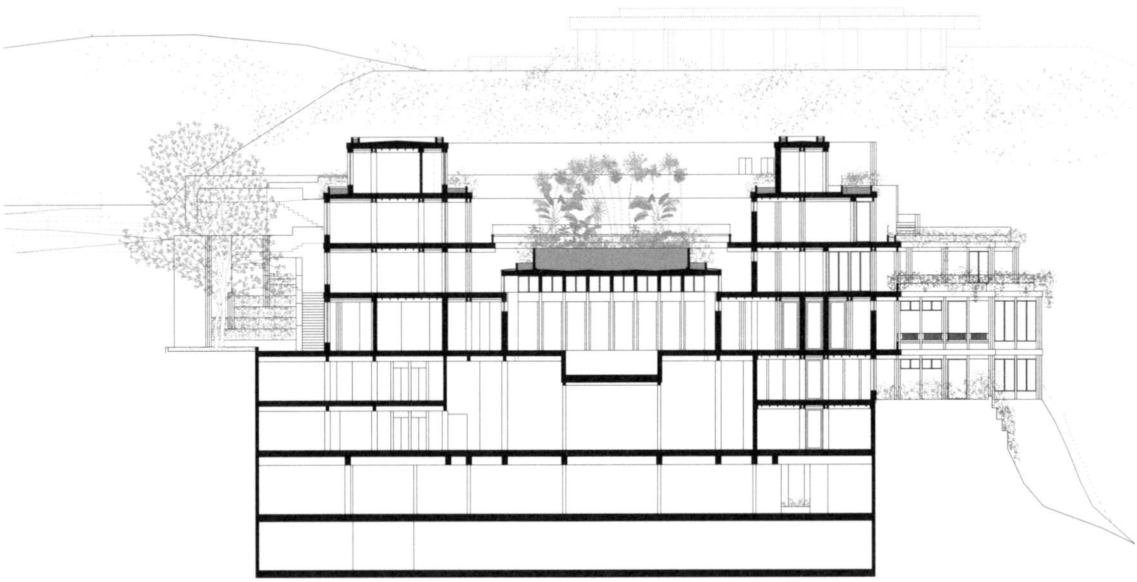

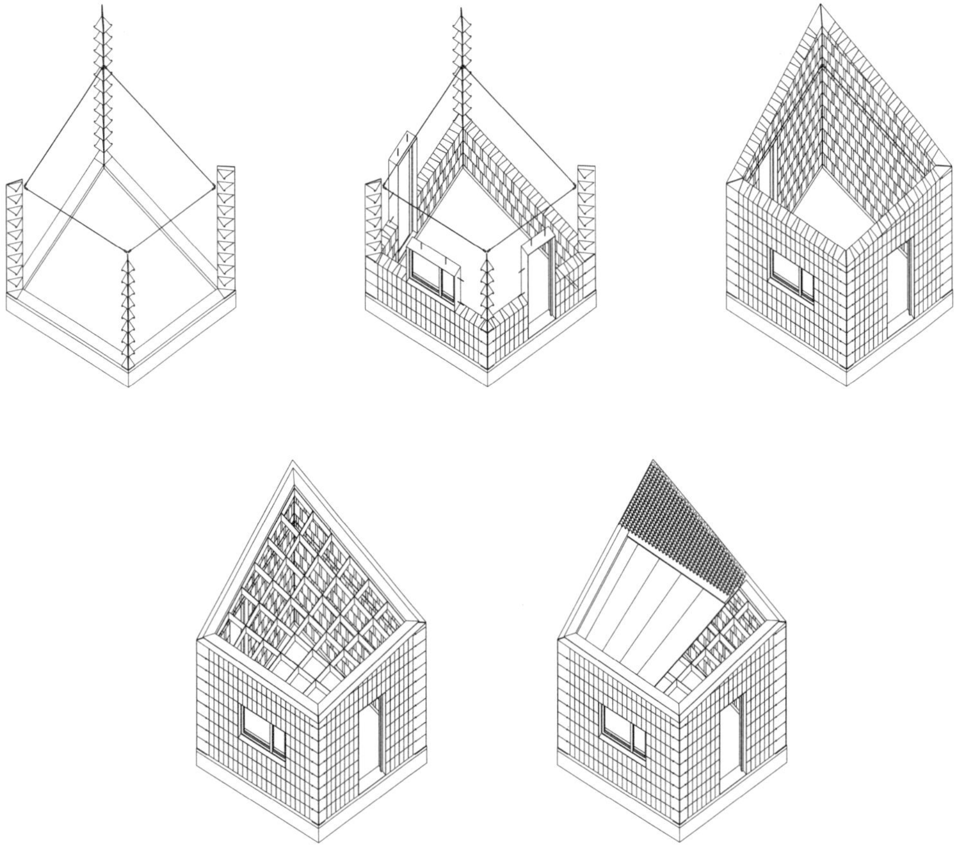

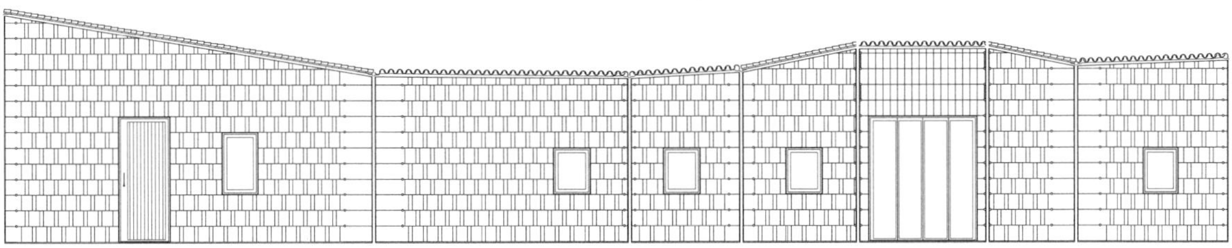

standard 12-18	n. 152+116+95+210=573
standard 12-6	n. 153+117+96+211=577
porte f 12-9	n. 18
porte f 12-15	n. 18

1a	n. 4	6a	n. 5	1b	n. 5	6b	n. 5
2a	n. 6	7a	n. 5	2b	n. 7	7b	n. 5
3a	n. 6	8a	n. 4	3b	n. 7	8b	n. 5
4a	n. 6			4b	n. 6		
5a	n. 6			5b	n. 6		

standard 12-18	n. 218+145+56+114+91=624
standard 12-6	n. 218+146+58+115+91=628
porte f 12-9	n. 11+2+2+8=23
porte f 12-15	n. 9+4+4+8=25

9a	n. 4	17a	n. 7	9b	n. 5	17b	n. 7
10a	n. 4	18a	n. 7	10b	n. 5	18b	n. 7
11a	n. 5	19a	n. 7	11b	n. 5	19b	n. 7
12a	n. 5	20a	n. 6	12b	n. 5	20b	n. 7
13a	n. 6			13b	n. 6		
14a	n. 6			14b	n. 6		
15a	n. 6			15b	n. 7		
16a	n. 6			16b	n. 7		

standard 12-18	n. 40+100=140
standard 12-6	n. 40+107=147
porte f 12-9	n. 5
porte f 12-15	n. 5
porte f 21	n. 8
porte f 22	n. 8

21a	n. 2	21b	n. 3
22a	n. 2	22b	n. 3
23a	n. 6	23b	n. 7
24a	n. 7	24b	n. 7

standard 12-18	n. 76+69+33+76=254
standard 12-6	n. 82+82+43+76=283
porte f 12-9	n. 8+8+4=20
porte f 12-15	n. 4+8+8+4=24

25a	n. 6	30a	n. 6	25b	n. 7	30b	n. 6
26a	n. 6	31a	n. 6	26b	n. 7	31b	n. 6
27a	n. 6	32a	n. 6	27b	n. 7	32b	n. 7
28a	n. 6	33a	n. 6	28b	n. 6	33b	n. 7
29a	n. 6	34a	n. 6	29b	n. 6	34b	n. 7

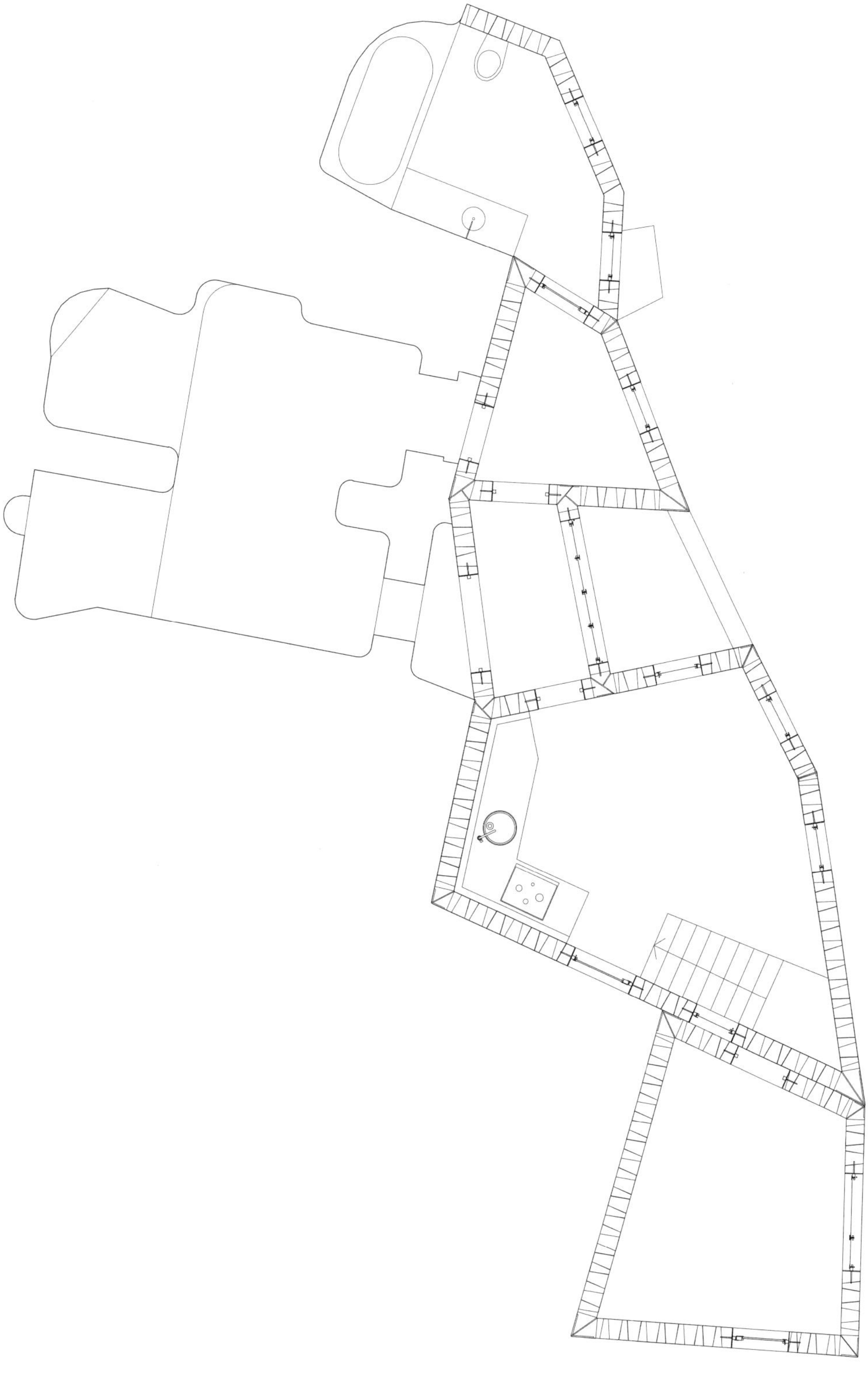

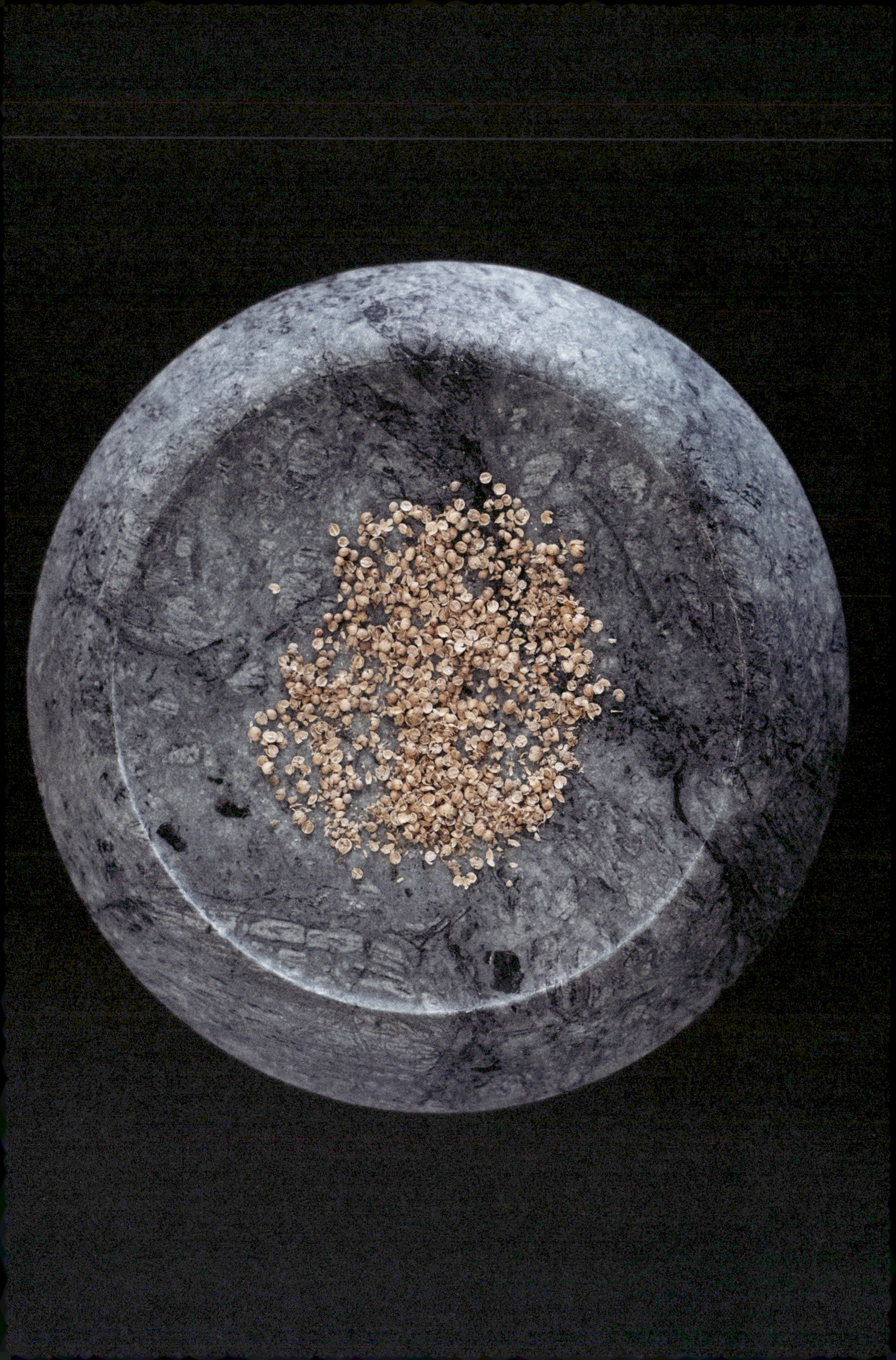

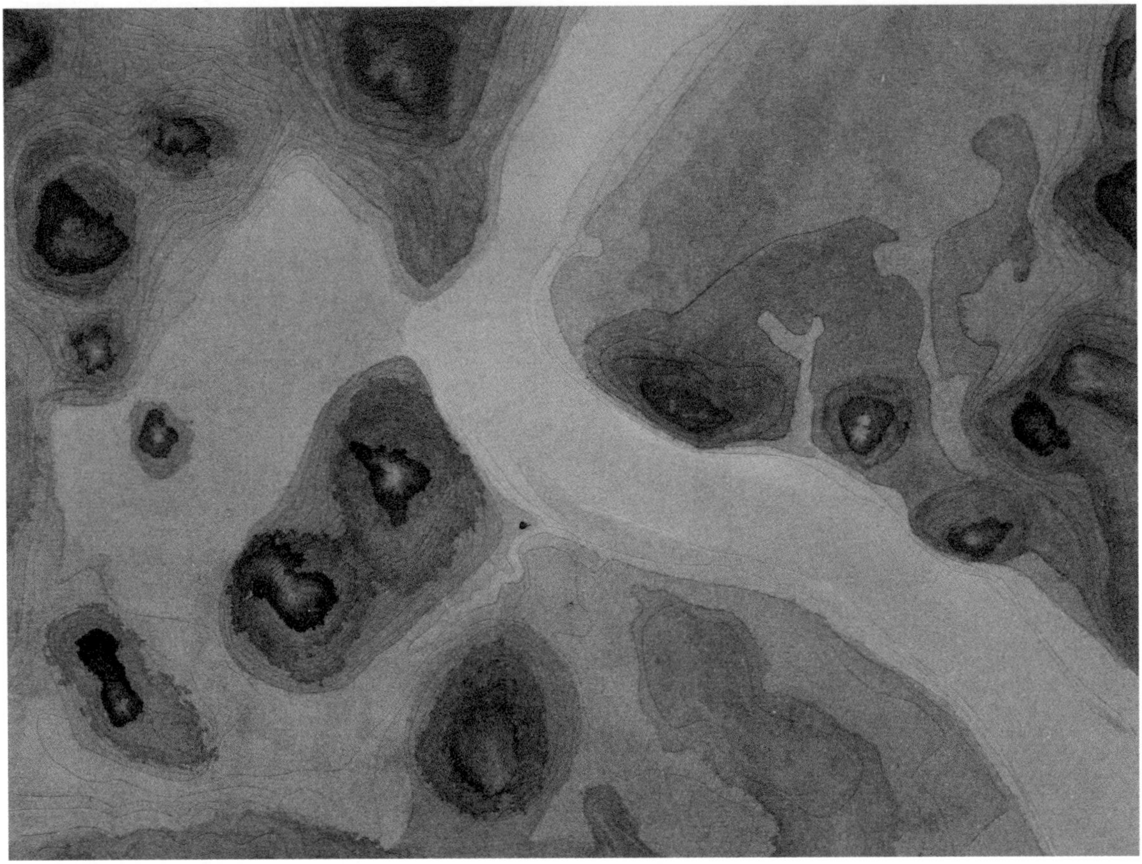

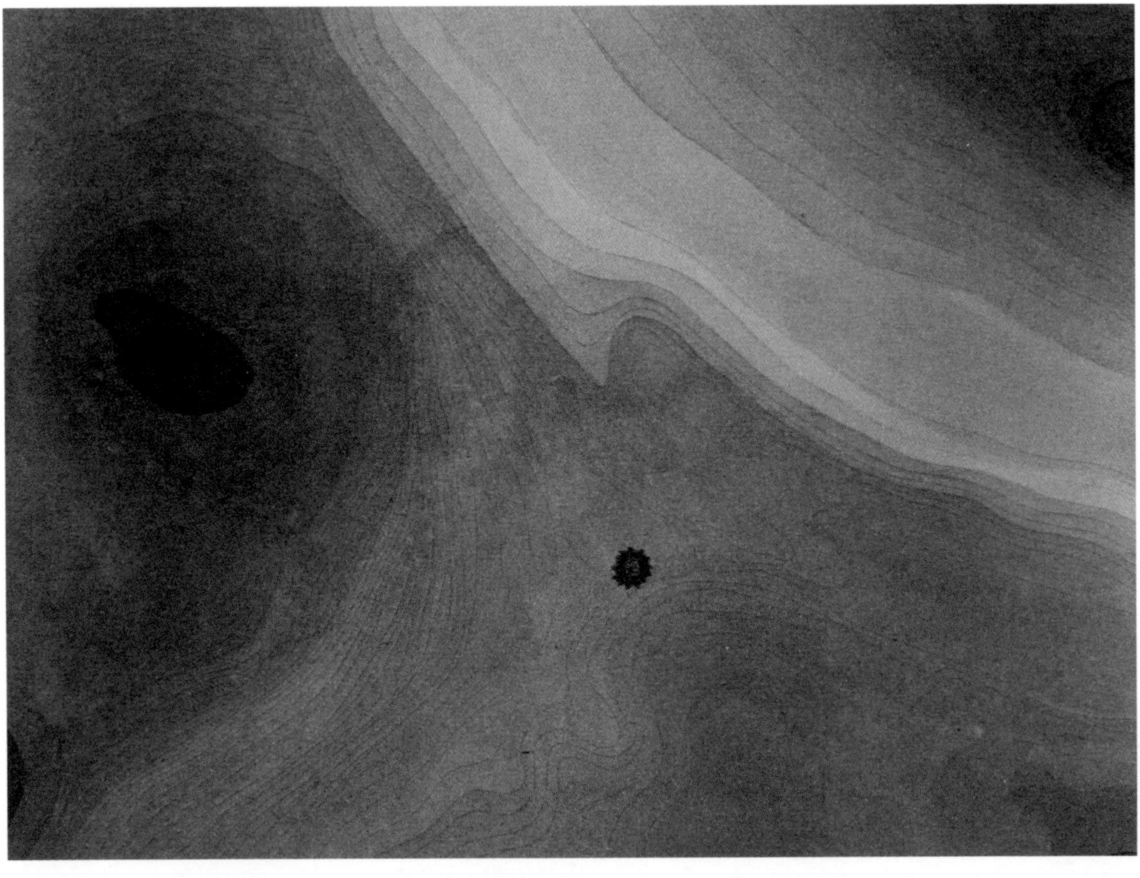

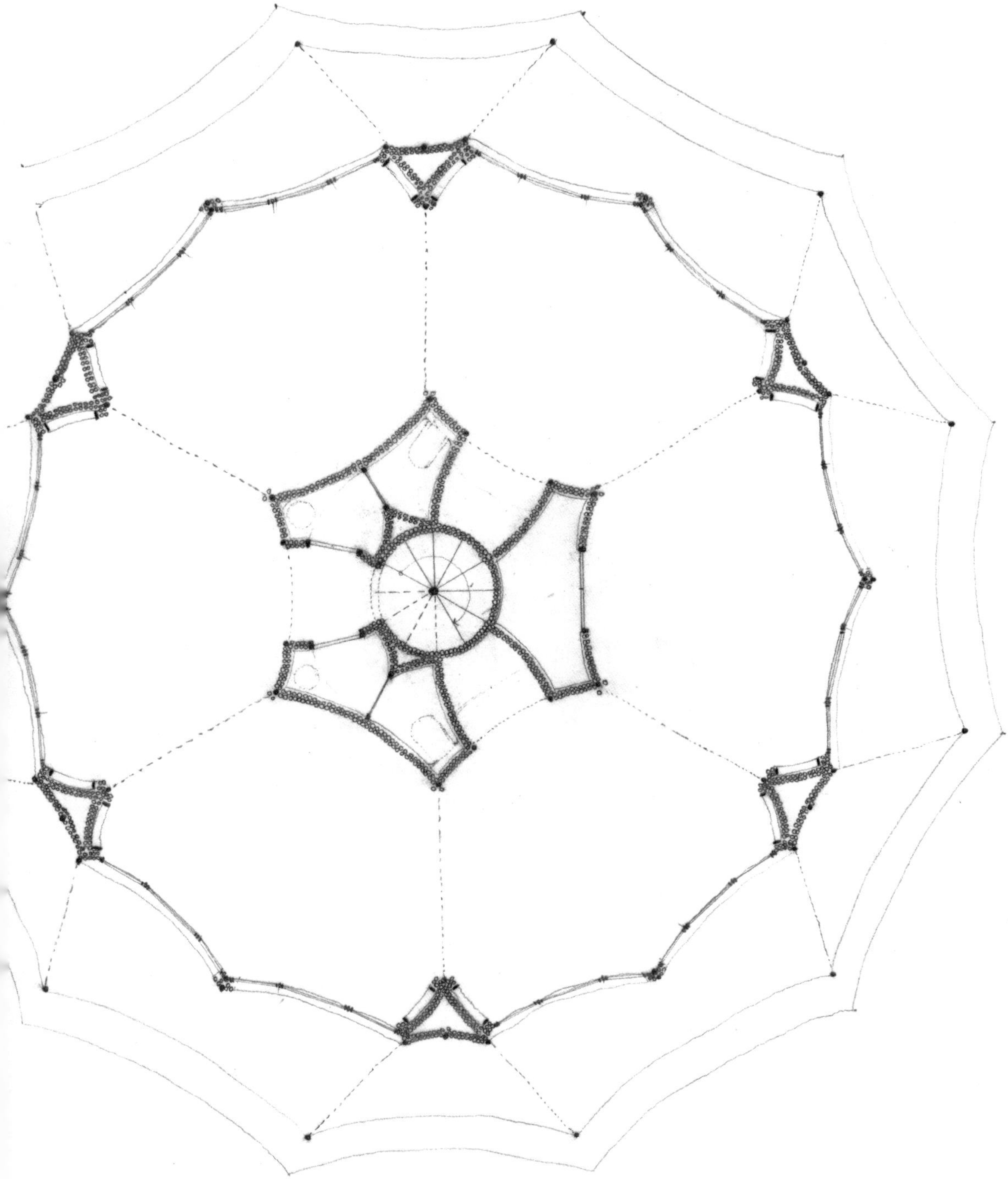

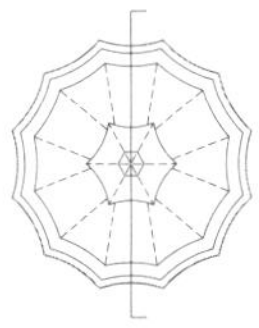

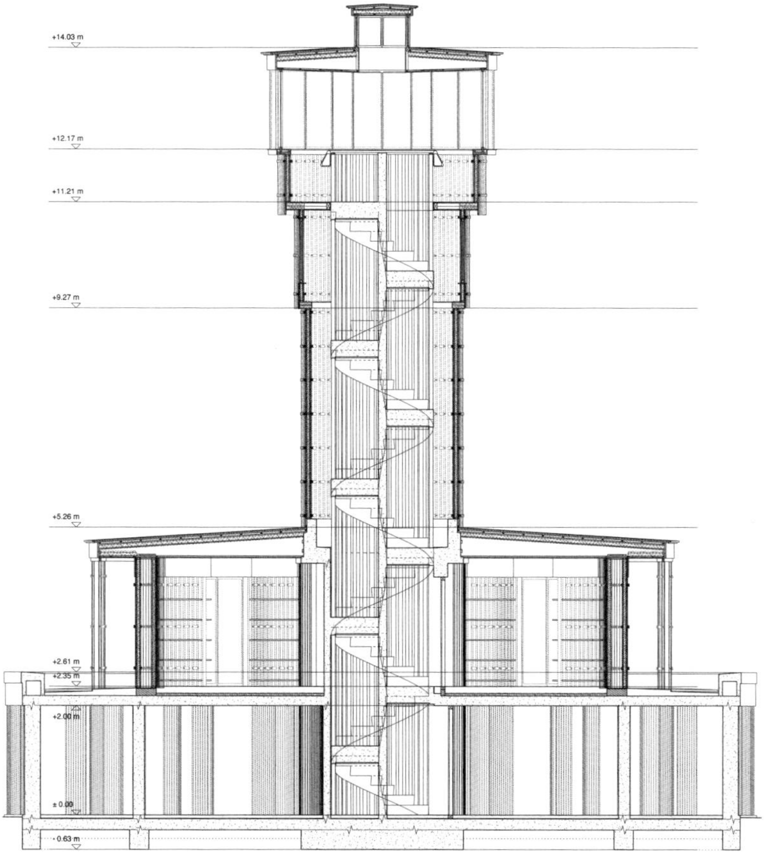
+14.03 m
+12.17 m
+11.21 m
+9.27 m
+5.26 m
+2.61 m
+2.35 m
+2.00 m
± 0.00
- 0.63 m

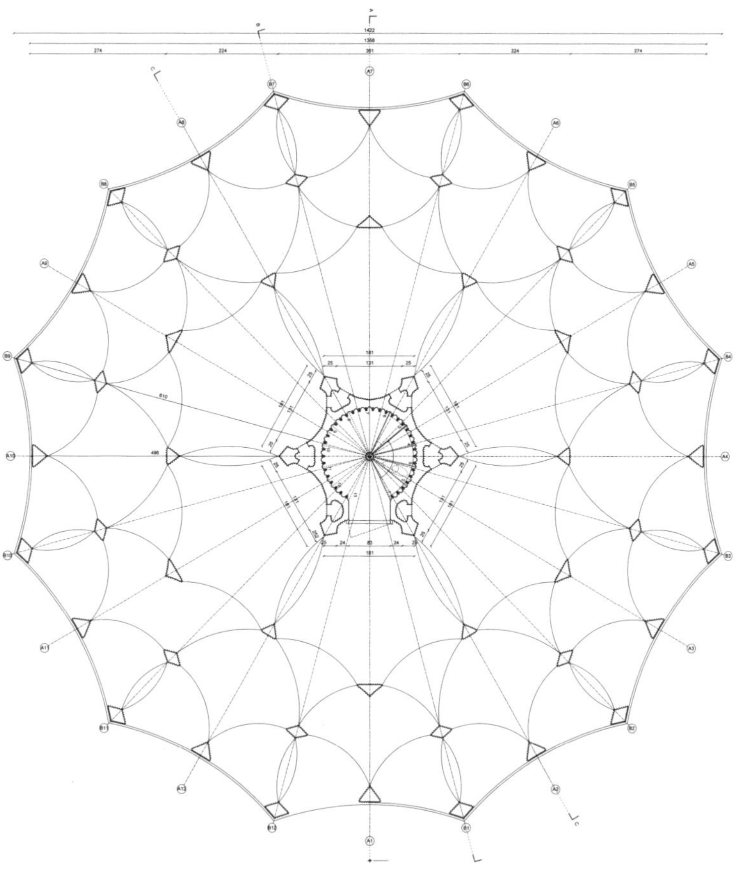

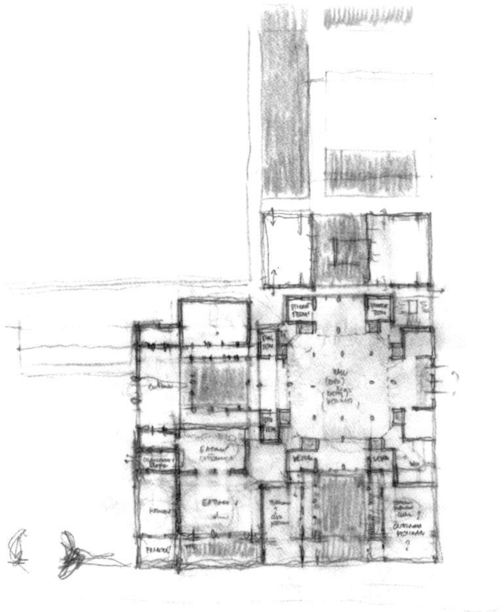

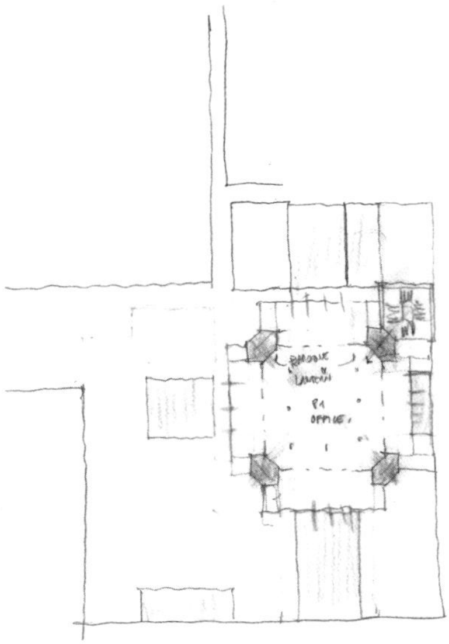

P1

~ 130 m2

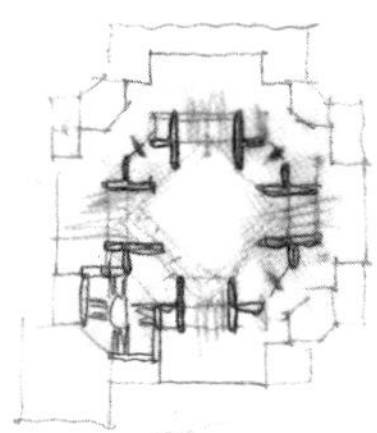

P2

~ 100 m2

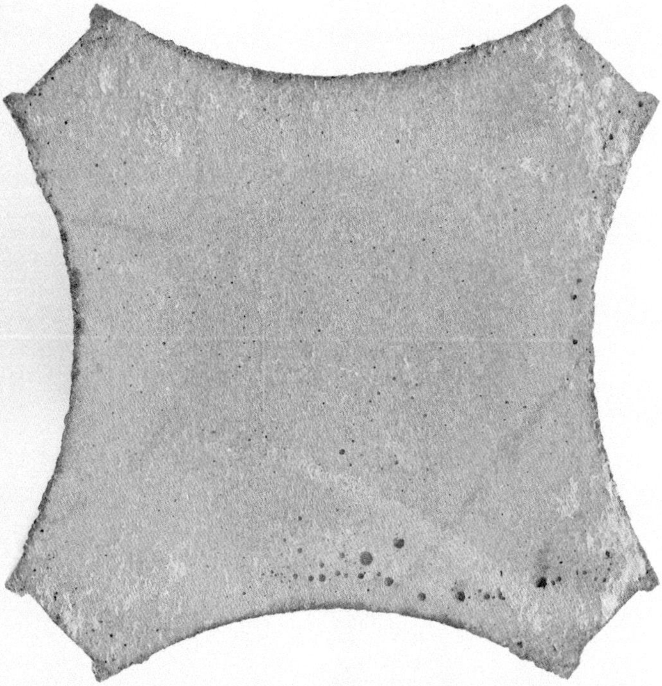

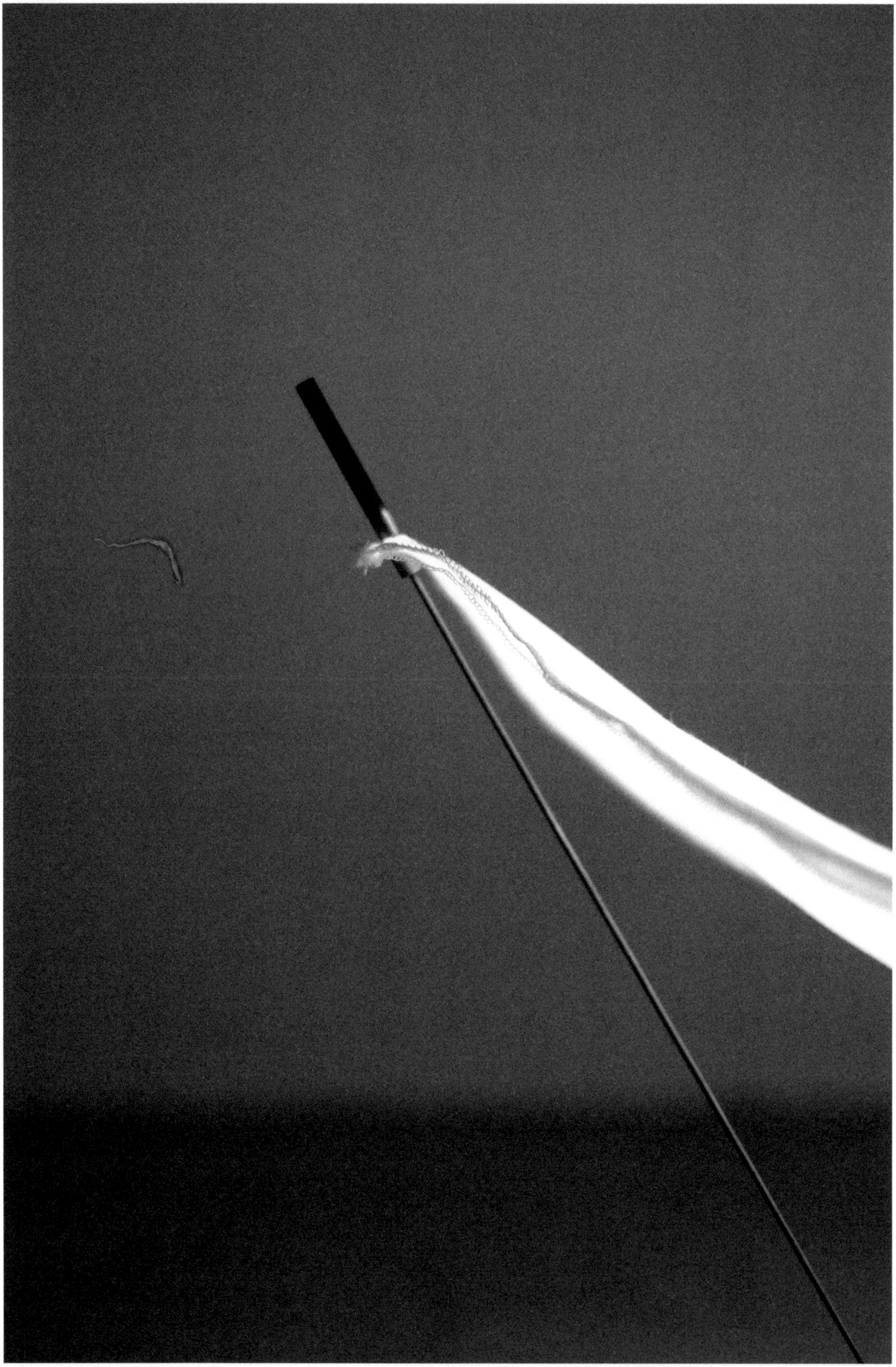

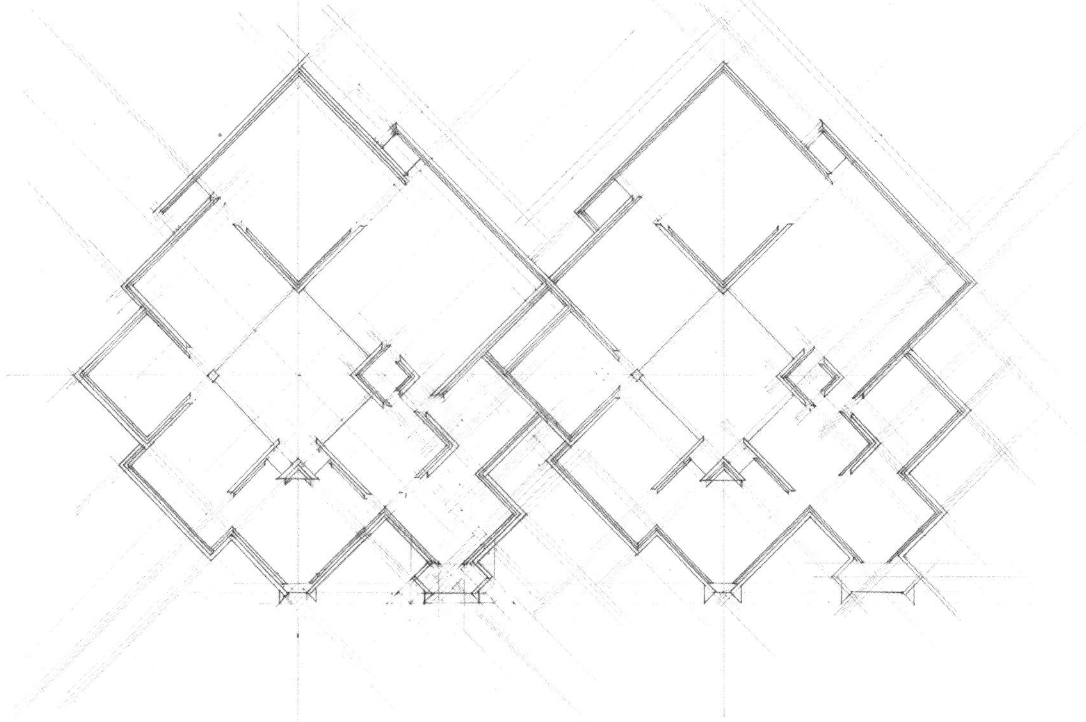

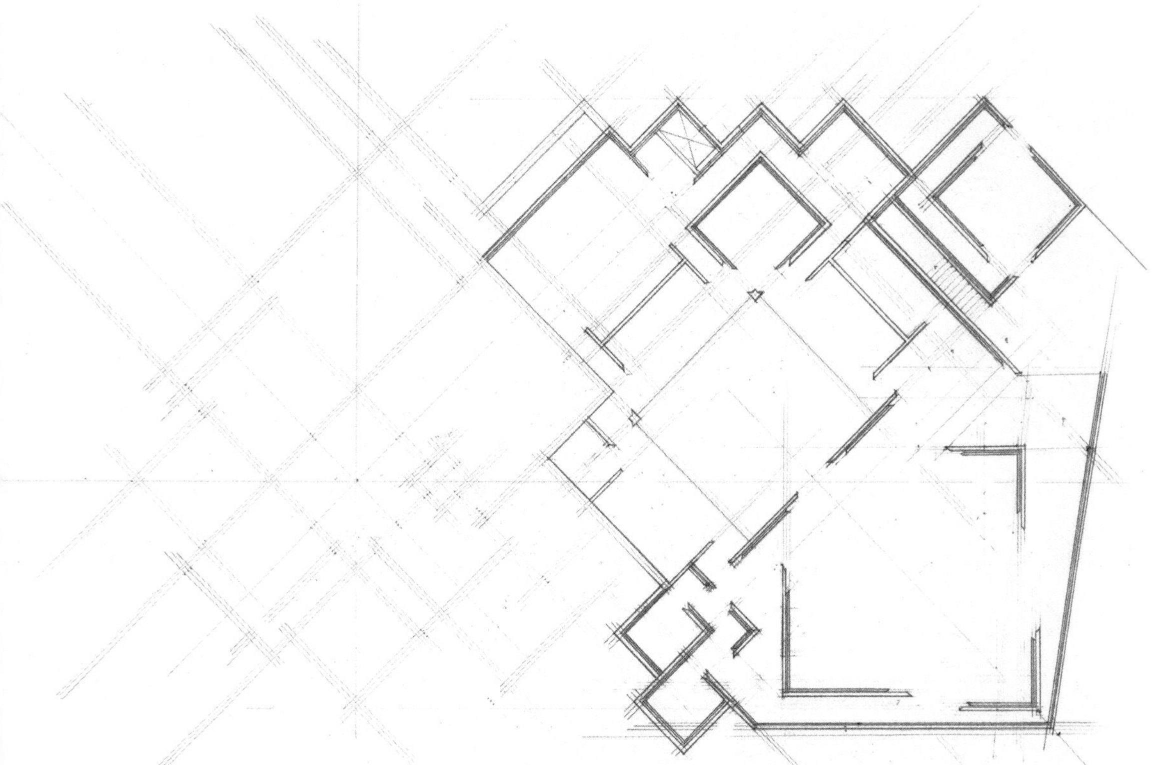

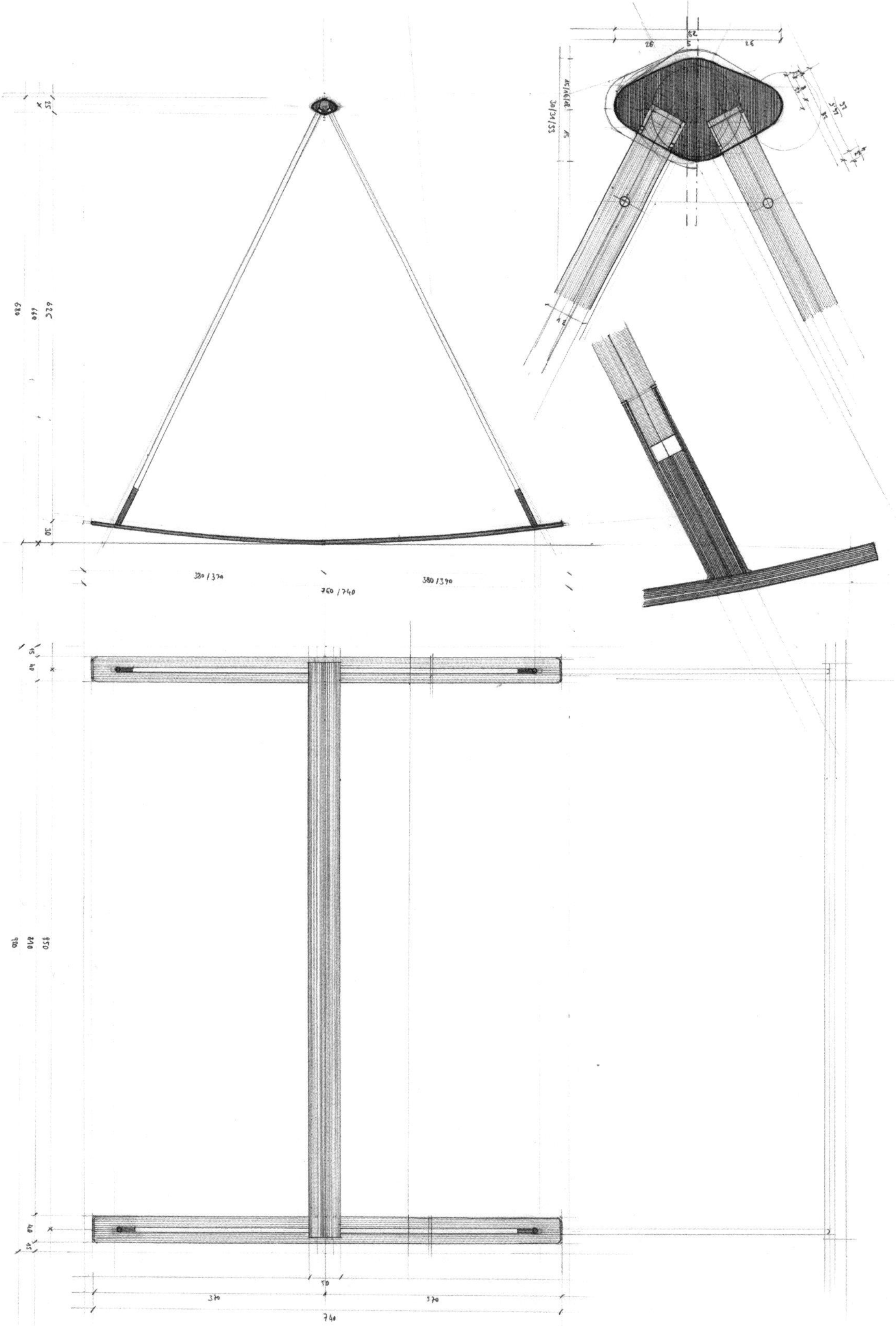

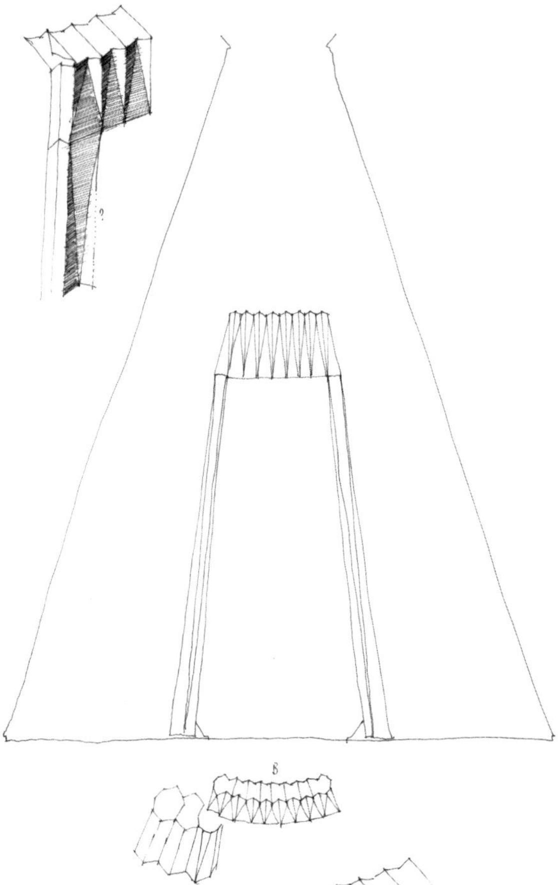
B

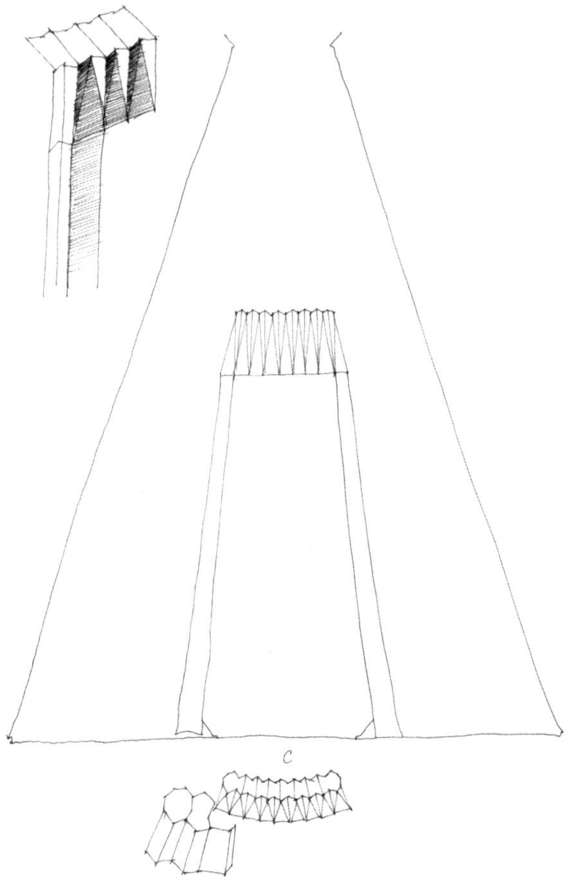
C

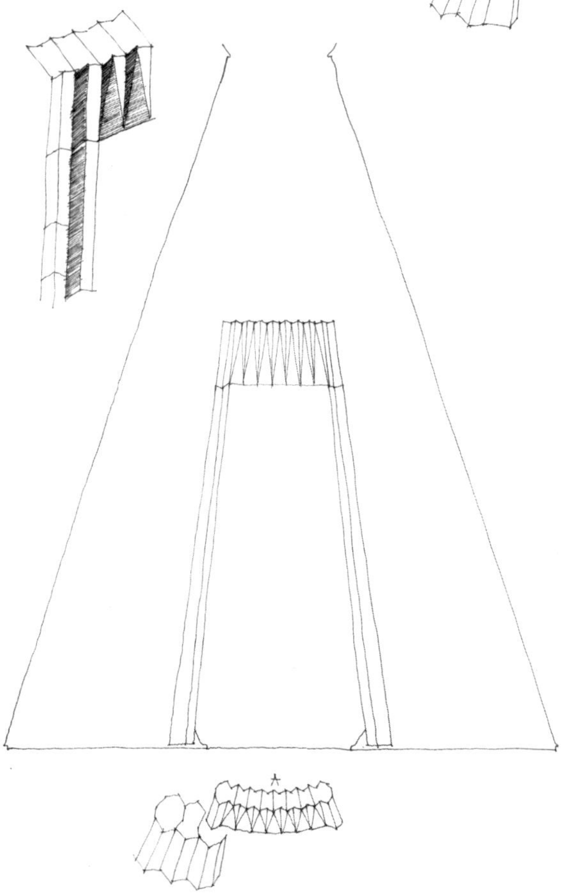
A

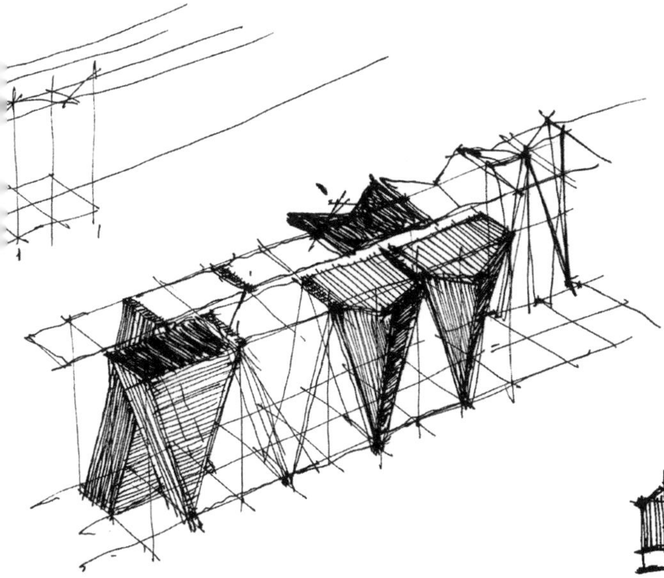

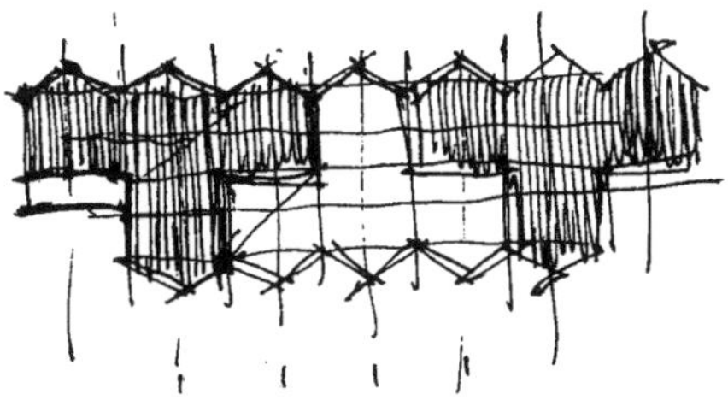

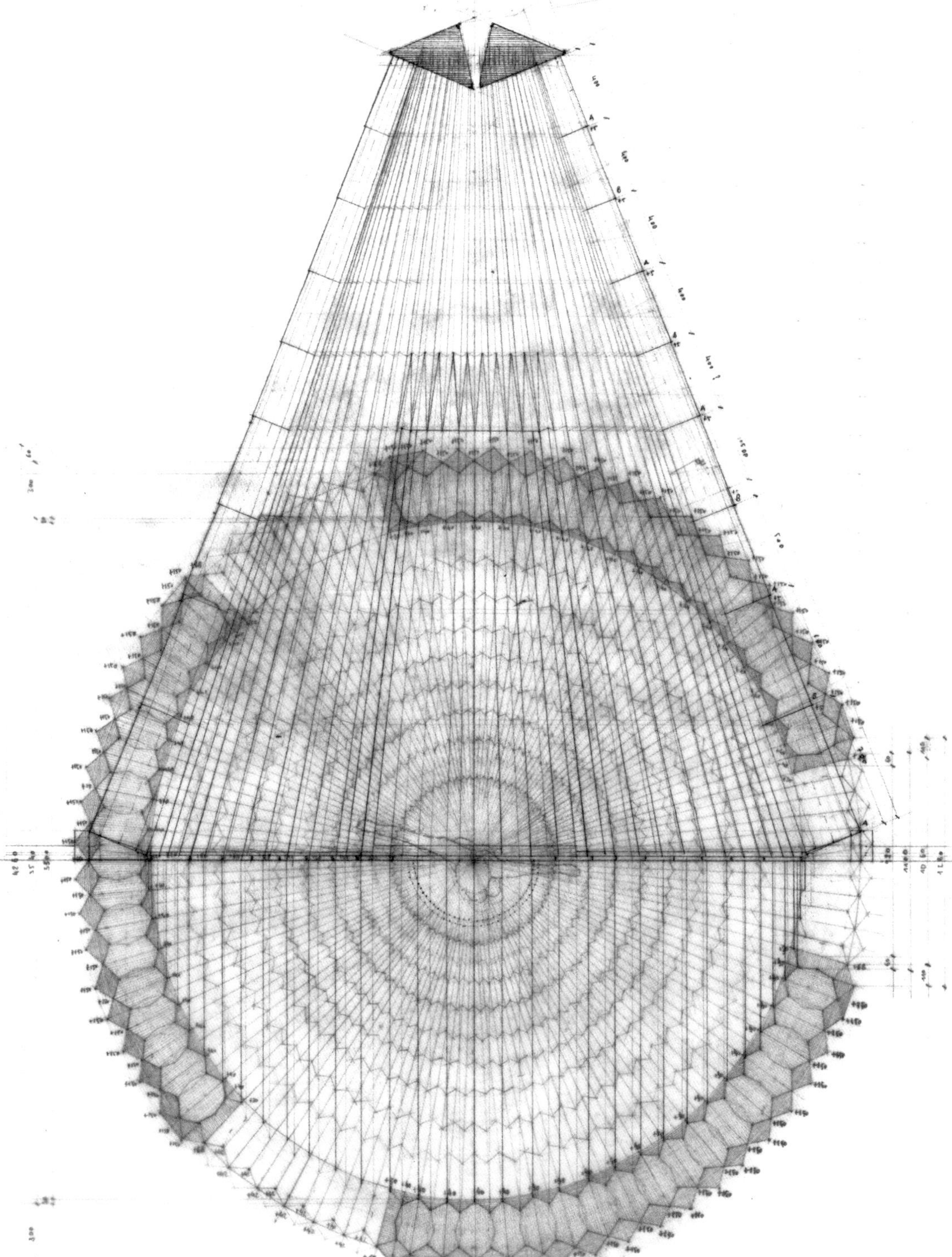

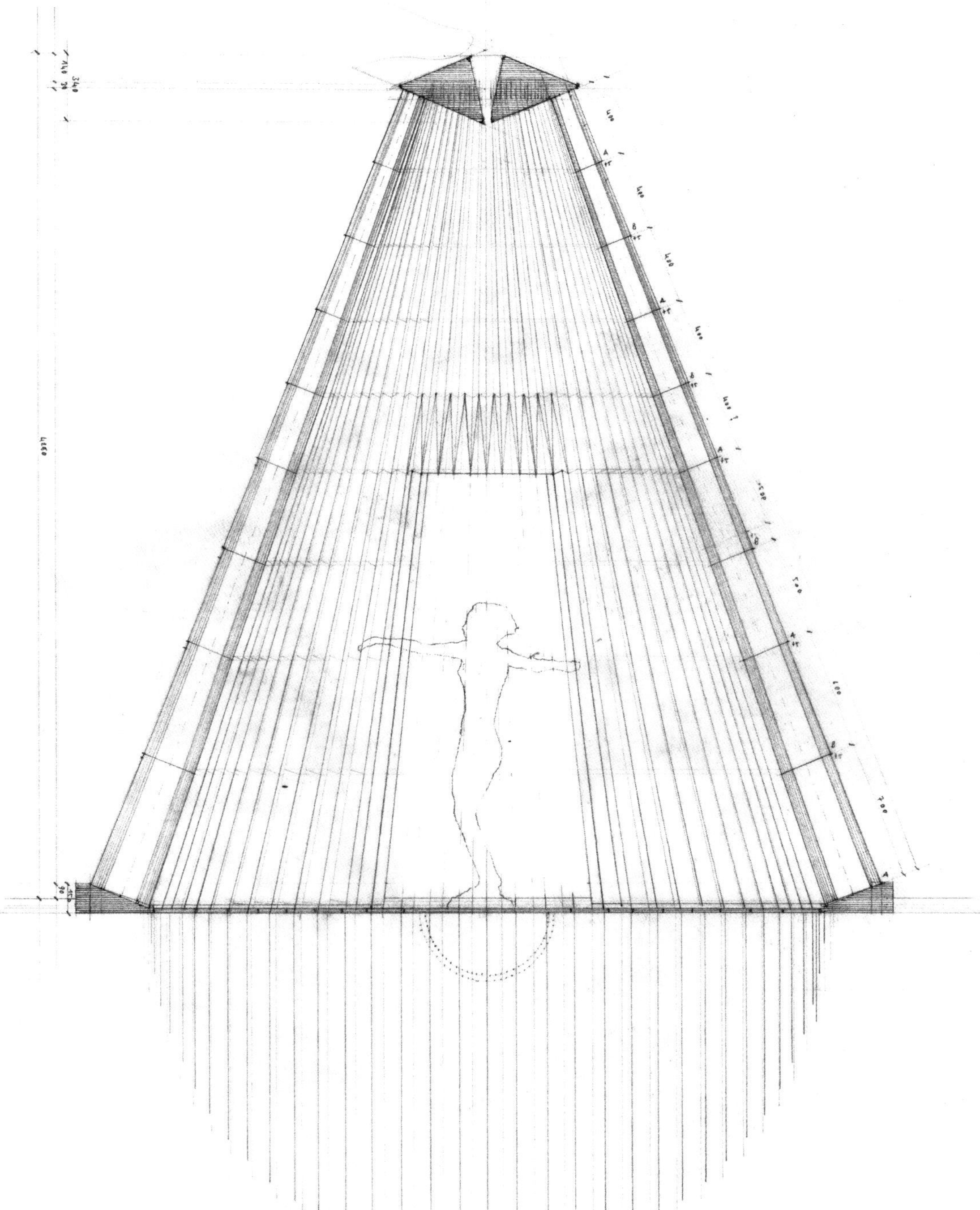

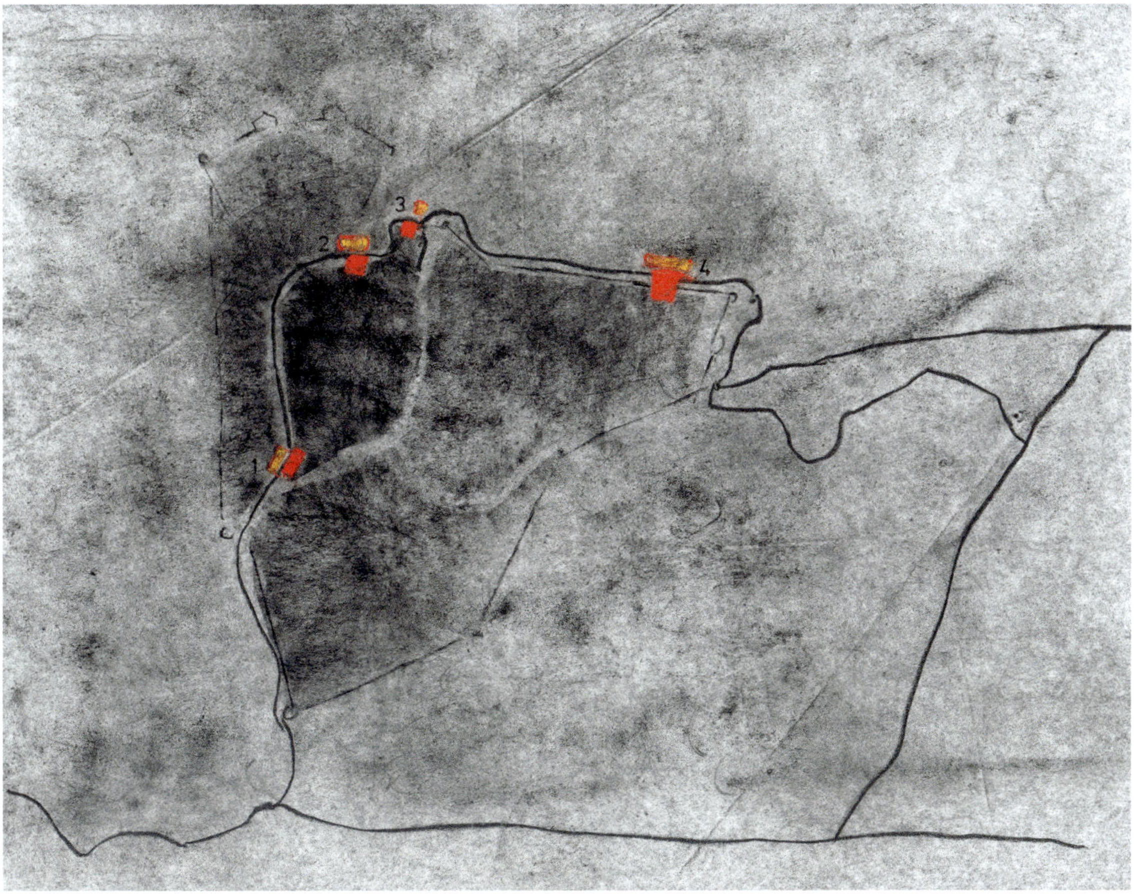
1
2
3
4

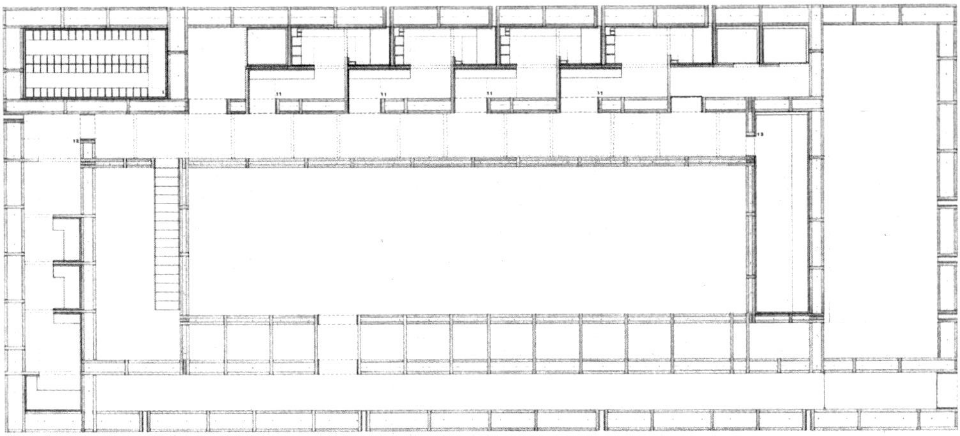

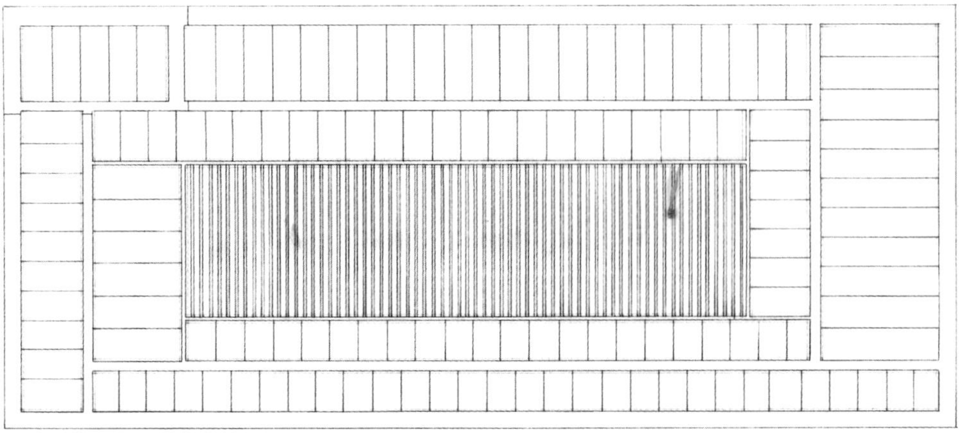

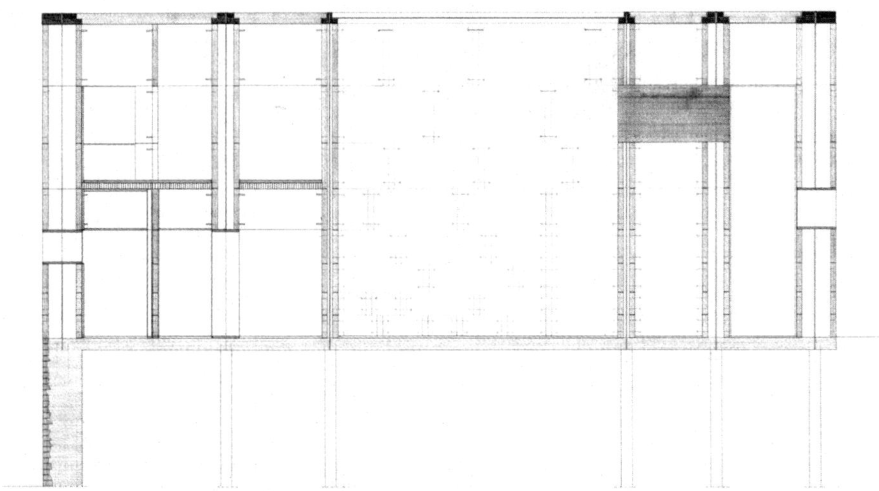

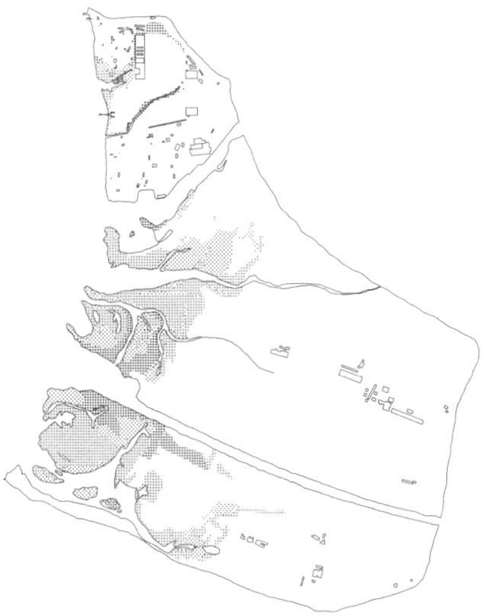

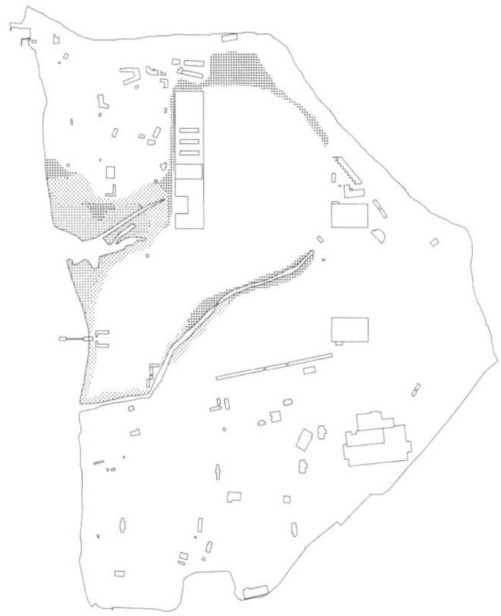

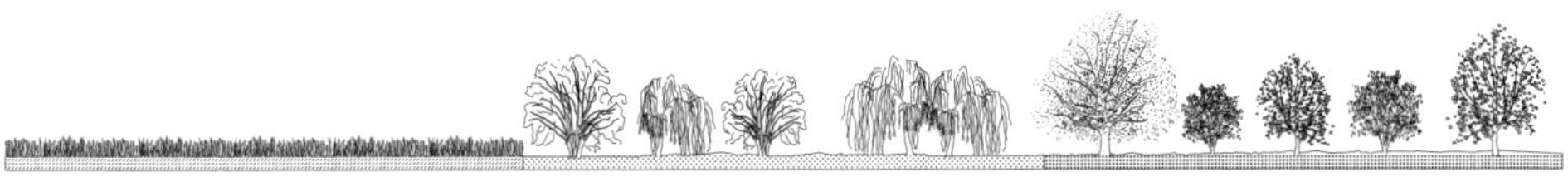

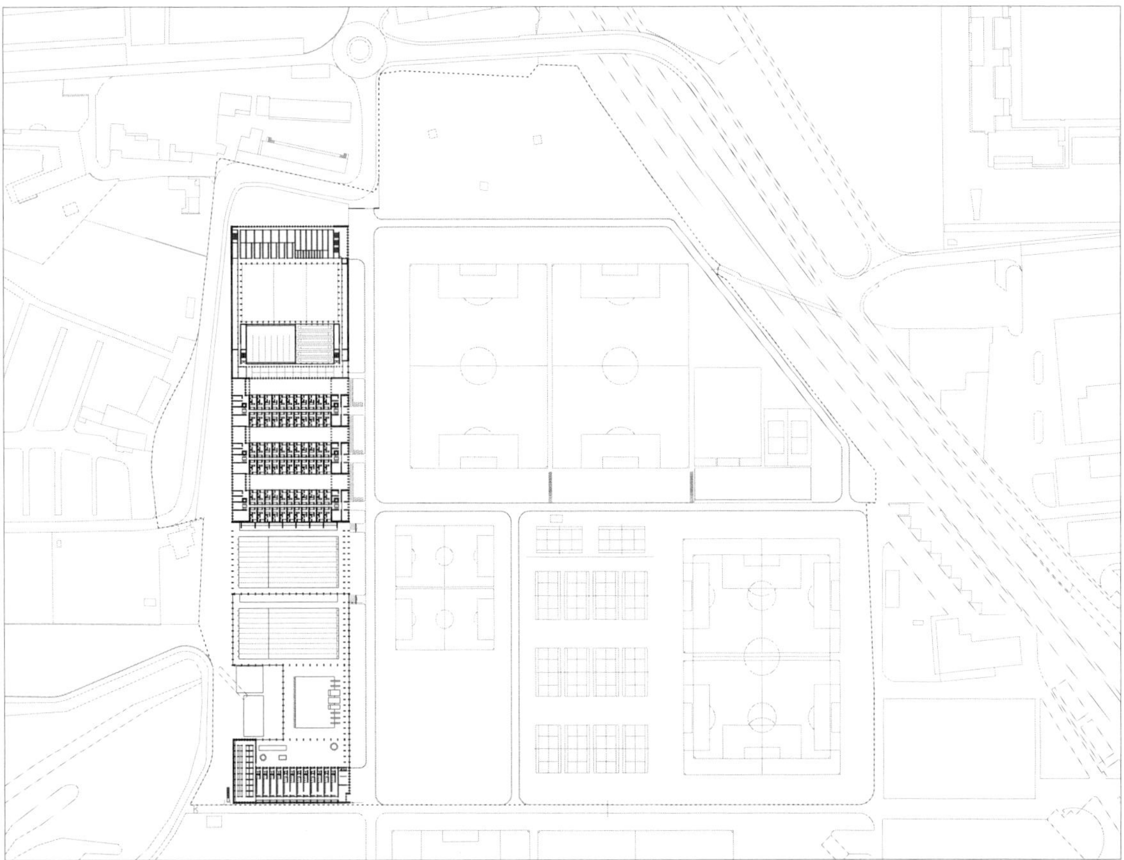

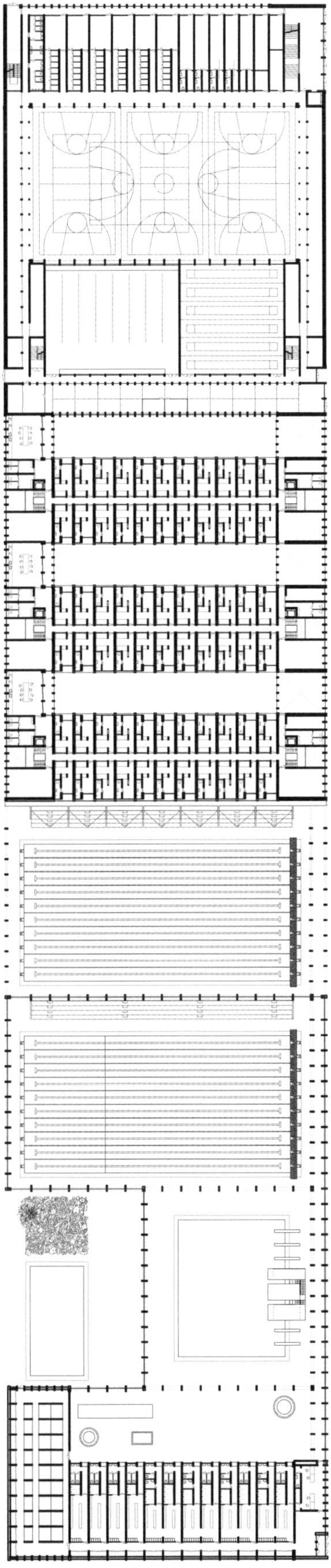

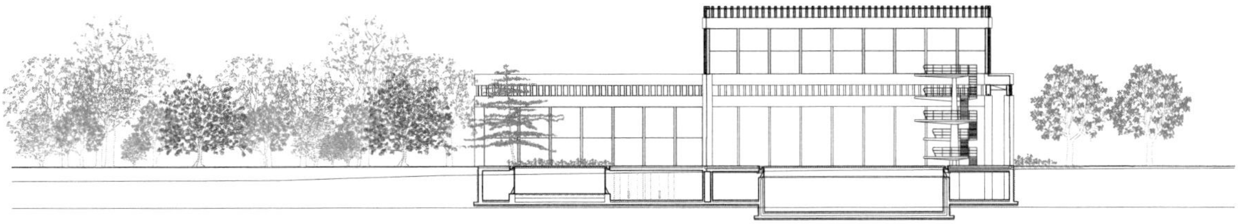

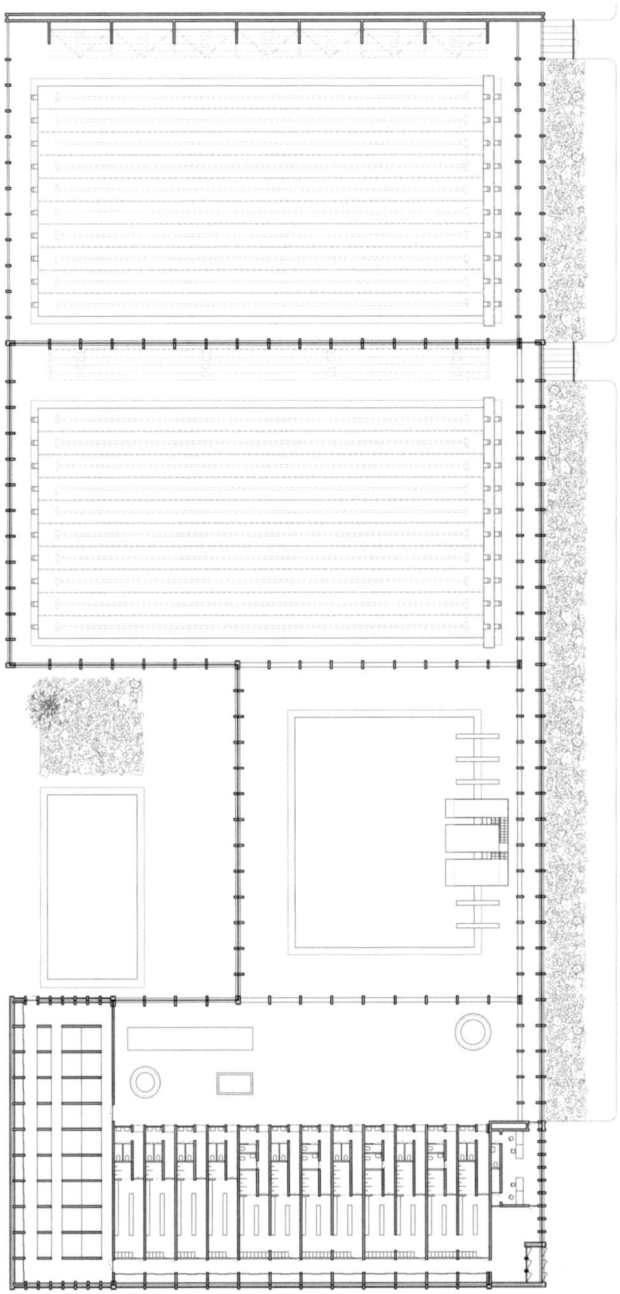

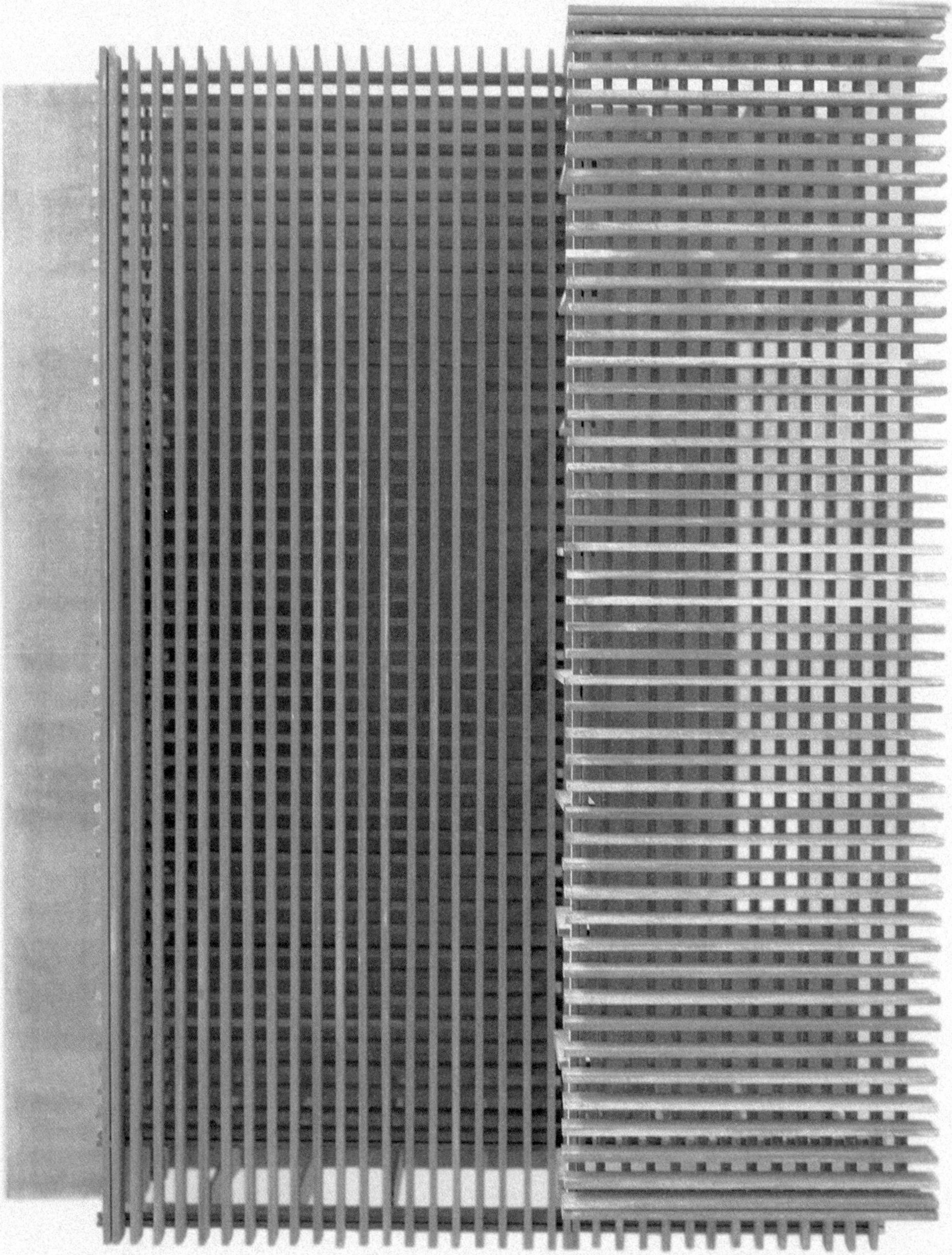

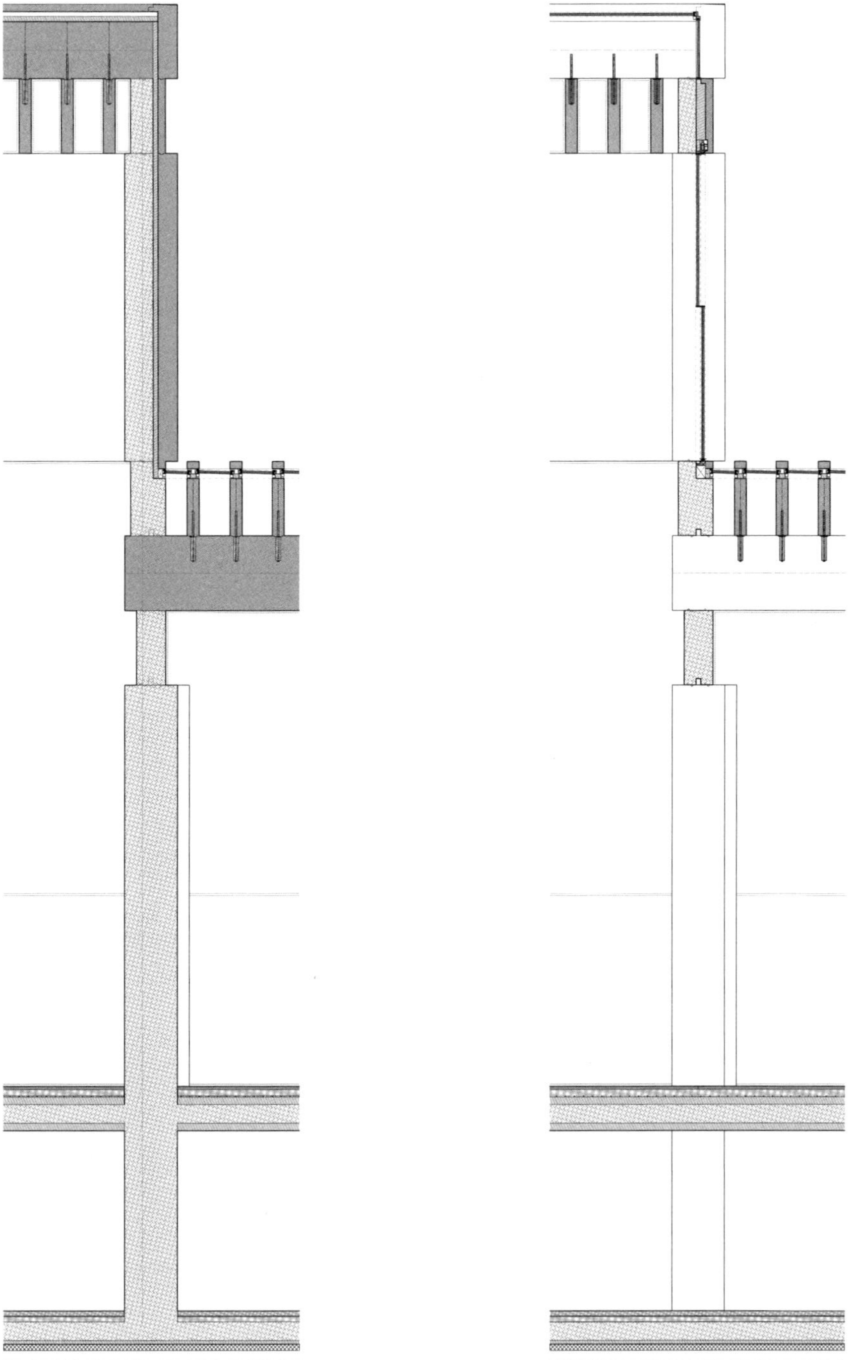

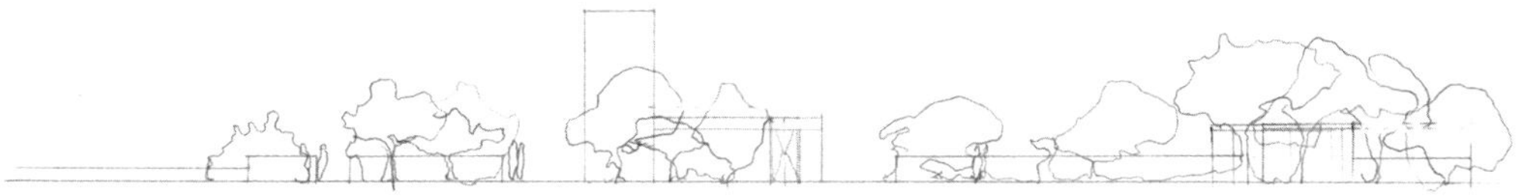

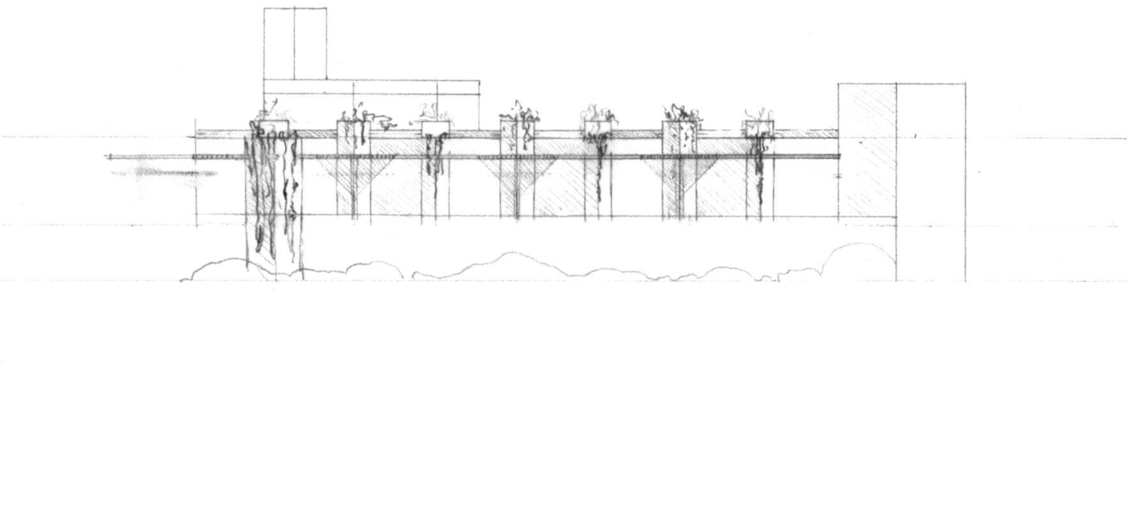

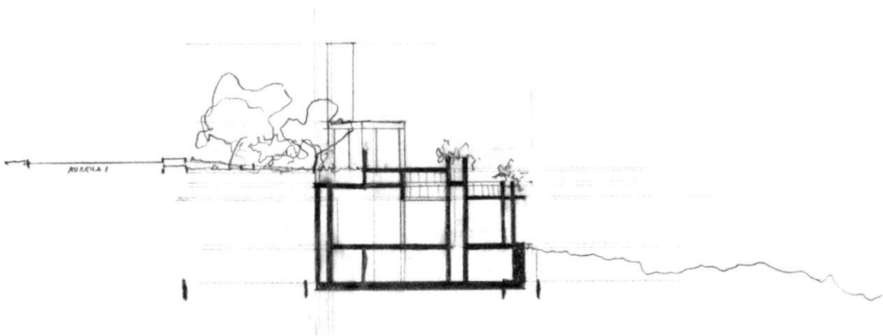

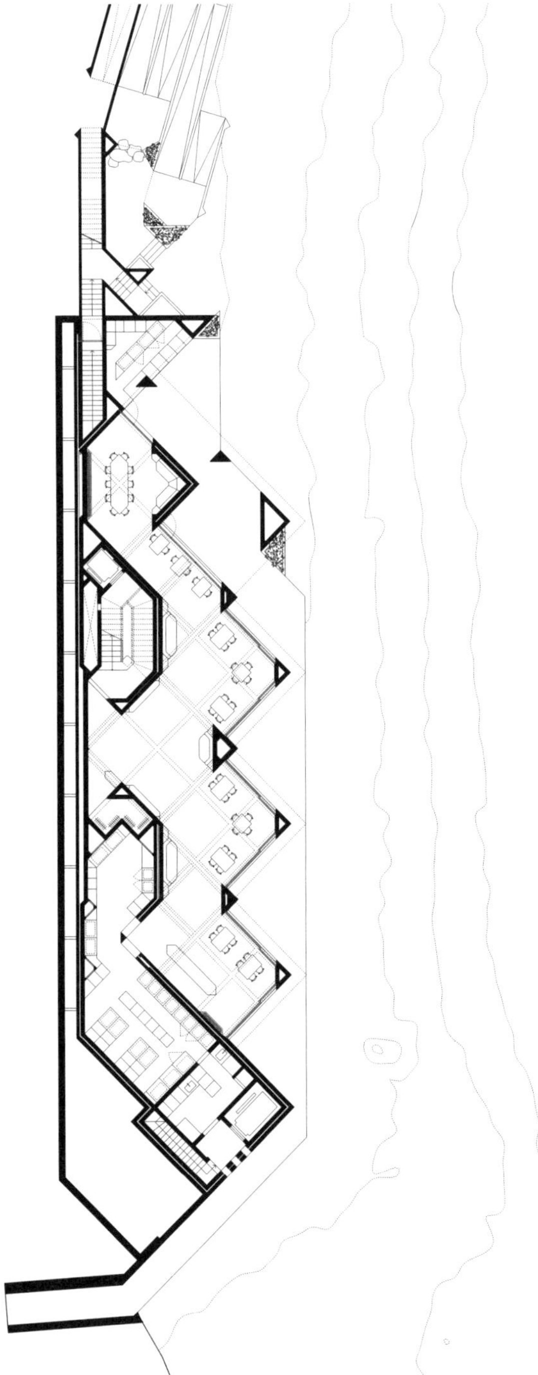

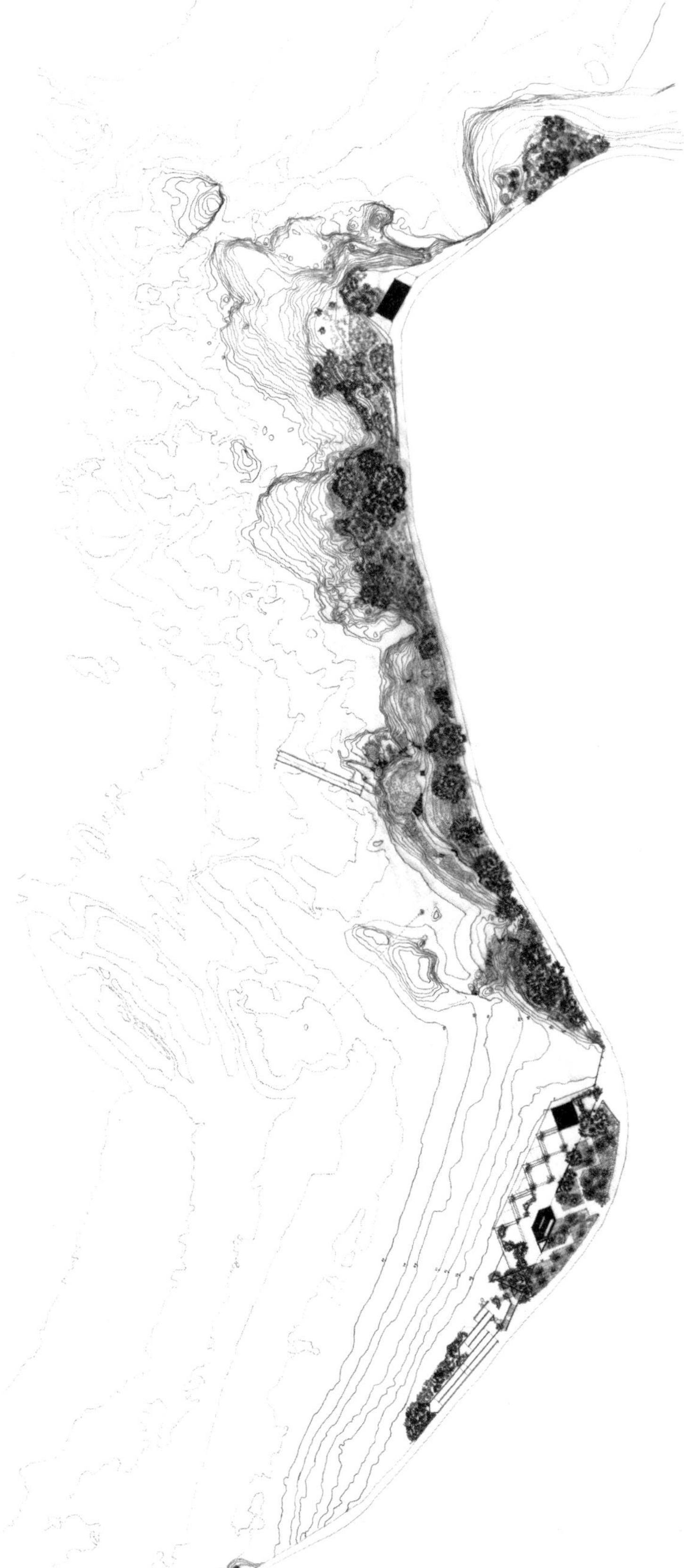

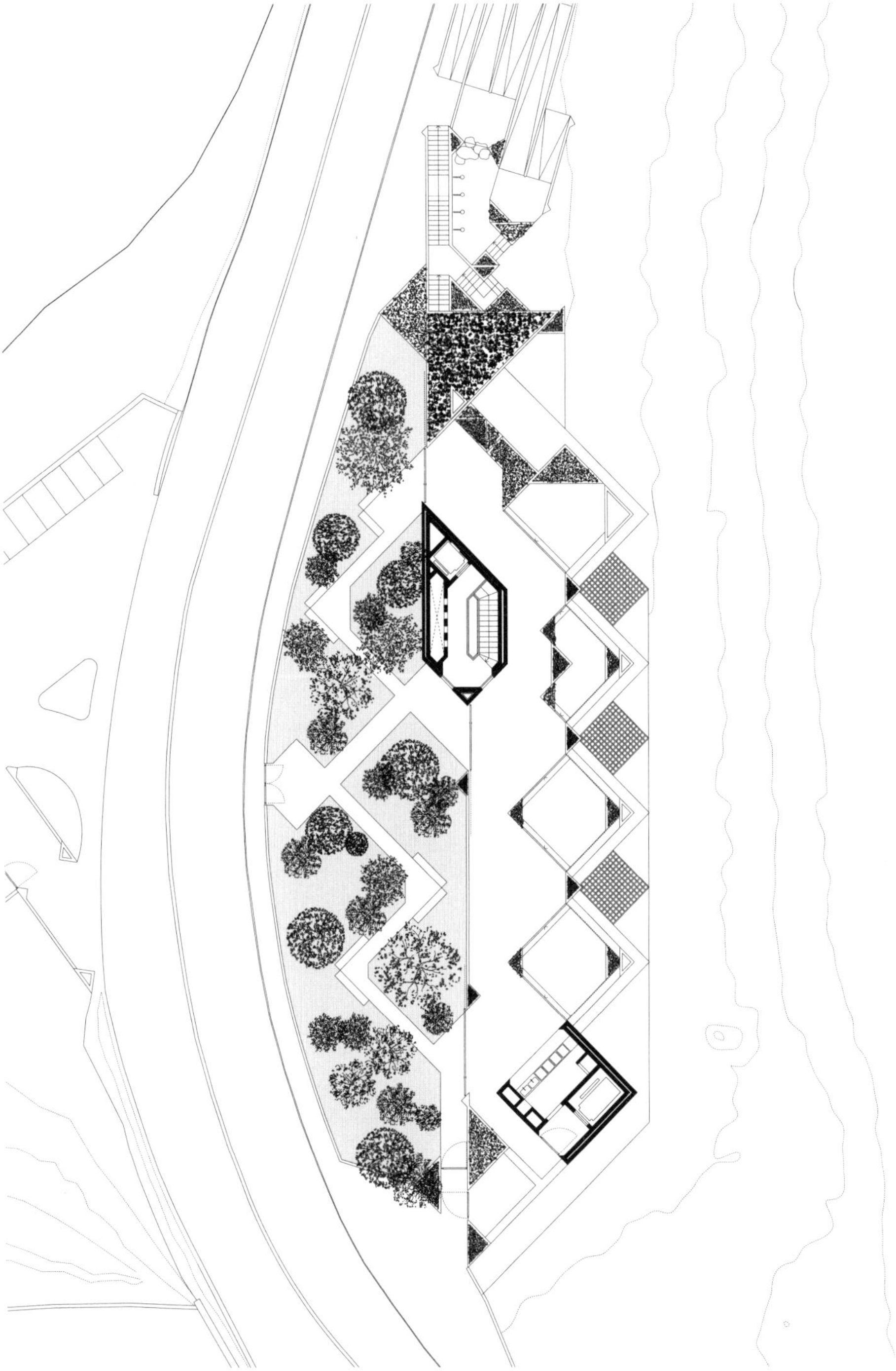

Q&A

with Elizabeth Hatz

and Ellis Woodman

ELLIS WOODMAN You describe a very singular position, Francesca. I would like to ask you about the significant moments that helped to formulate the kind of thinking you set out in this lecture. I am interested in this impulse towards making architecture that is rooted in a particular condition but is also evocative of other times and places. I was reminded of two other architects I know you admire, Jørn Utzon and Sverre Fehn, and their visits to Morocco and, in Utzon's case, to Mexico, Iran and China. Could you say something about this engagement with architecture from outside the European tradition?

FRANCESCA TORZO My first experience of travelling was through literature and books. As a child, I was often ill and read a lot. *One Hundred and One Nights*, a version earlier than *One Thousand and One Nights*, was one of my favourite texts. It is a layered body of life experiences stretching across a vast time span as it comes from oral culture. Next to this travelling of the mind, I also spent time travelling with my mother and father. With my mother especially, I shared a passion for wandering in archaeological museums. I used to help her at the Civic Museum of Padova, our home city. Here, I would encounter so many countries, finding gems from cultures far away, compiling stone arrows, archiving all these finds with tiny notes. This meant we observed a lot. At the time, I wasn't aware that I had a professor explaining to me – obviously in very simplified terms – that humans had travelled from one region to another, carrying with them their skills in cutting stones and so on. So, returning to your question, distant cultures are indeed a familiar companion, even though I've lived my life in Europe. Many cultures are so close.

ELIZABETH HATZ There are certain words and concepts that seem very important in this text: 'urban *portamento*', 'non-authorial wisdom', or the kind of reconfirmation of an identity that lies beyond a particular architectural language. You detect deep enduring urban structures when you describe how you relate to a place, a reading that is almost archaeological, geological even. You read the landscape as a cultural artefact, a place where humans have been working, living and loving for so long. For me, though, what comes back again and again is the title of your lecture, 'Building Correctly': you're interested in the tectonic, in construction, and this is deeply linked to the spatial sensitivity I see in your work. Villa di Plinio is not only connected to the landscape, but is totally a cultural construct, with roots in the nineteenth century – from Schinkel you borrow a thin, delicate kind of structure holding an order that sets up an interdependence between what is inside and what is outside. I find it fascinating that you travel through reading – you're one of the best-read architects I know – and yet there is another layer of close observation which comes out in your drawings, in your little models that pick up on both geologies, the *portamento* of a place combined with the thinness, delicacy and ingenuity of a structure. Because you observe constantly.

FT What you say makes sense to me. The other night I watched Michelangelo Antonioni's *Blow-Up* again, and I was struck by a scene showing mime artists driving their jeep up the steps and around the Smithsons' The Economist Building: it resembled Pienza with surprising precision. I couldn't swear the dimensions are the same, but they show the same posture within the city: you have a square, which is a stage, and the square isn't defined by a single figure; rather, it is articulated. From this stage you overlook either the urban landscape of roads and façades of

London or the cultivated lands of Tuscany. Even if in London the scene is built in concrete, it offers a similar gentleness in expression to the Italian piazza. It is very difficult to reconstruct all the physical or mental travels of someone, but to me it is surprising how precise such similarities are, even if not exact in terms of parameter or figure.

EH It's interesting that you mention Alison and Peter Smithson, because when I was reading your text, I made a little note – 'I'd like a drawing here' – because you describe very particular, extremely refined structural moments in your buildings. Alison and Peter Smithson worked with little drawings they called 'ideograms', something between a diagram and an idea. When I read your text, I long for your drawings. Your way of working is so mysterious, and I think it's extremely rare to find an architect who has such a talent for structure today. When we talk about your references and your connection to travel through books or with your mother, I think of Franco Albini: I can't help it because of the tradition, in Italian architecture, to establish continuities within the project of modernity. My question then is, How do you register these thoughts and observations?

FT I constantly keep in mind the question of how we can fabulate with our minds without being tricked. How can we get to the core of something that doesn't merely echo one's own point of view, but can be meaningful for people we don't know, so that they can have narrating voices too. Among personal observations, how do we discern those that can have meaning and narrative for others? I was fortunate to see Utzon's Sydney Opera House in person and I found it humanistic more than iconic. All the tiled surfaces are real, at hand and somehow domestic; there is nothing abstract. The acoustics are fabulous, and the building has a civic theatrical performance, similar to Hans Scharoun's Berliner Philarmonie, where there are multiple ways of gathering and encountering people. Observing these curving lines also reminds me of Alberto Ponis, who died recently. He also used to observe elements in nature and translate their behaviours. If I look at the leaf, it is fascinating that such a thin structure can take such fierce wind loads. How can it be so intelligent? I try to understand how I can learn from its logic and principles; at the same time, I don't want to make a shell, flower or cloud. I want to make a building.

EW Your work invariably seeks a sense of continuity with a pre-existing architectural condition, but I wonder to what extent you see your work as a model for a modern vernacular. Clearly these are buildings that establish a critical position in relation to the vast bulk of industrialized building production, but they aren't easy buildings to build – they present a level of technical refinement that isn't readily replicated.

FT That is such a relevant question to reflect on. I don't have anything against industrial components, but I may recognize that they are reduced in comparison to the first lines of production. This needs to be challenged. Components today are often flat, while most of the building elements have been composed, for centuries or millennia, into architectures with a plurality of shadows and reliefs. In this window behind me, the few millimetres of shadow make an articulation where the eye can rest. If it was a totally flat assembly, the scale would be overwhelming and disorienting. So, for me, it's pretty much a matter of scale.

EW I was in Majorca recently visiting the Utzon House at Can Lis and it was fascinating to see, forty to fifty years on, the extent to which that building has become a sort of model for a whole generation of Majorcan architects who developed types of social housing on the basis of Utzon's tectonic language. Given the kinds of jobs you've got at the moment, one might suggest that you're operating in a more rarefied realm of exceptional buildings, and I wonder to what extent you feel at ease with this situation.

FT To get a chance to design social housing, you have to win a competition, and I lose competitions; I've literally never had the chance to get a social housing project. But I can honestly say that I'm very fond of anonymity. Cities need the anonymity of the dwellings that make most of their body. They should have a certain degree of repetitiveness which enables one to rest, to not be continuously alerted by individual events. There are so many strands related to this idea. One is societal: a whole part of society and social media communication enhances individuality. This is a seed of modernity that has become dominant within architectural practices, where we are asked to perform individually, often through competitions which reward the uniqueness of a building. On the other hand, I grew up in a context that valued a sense of community. It was there when I was born, and today I see through my students that it can be regained. Given these contradictions, achieving a dignifying sense of anonymity is very difficult, as those providing the economic means need to make a stand, need to be recognized. This poses questions on how to build: there is no shared whisper on how a house should be. How relevant is this subject of recognizability? In this sense, I'm very happy with where I live and work, in Genoa, because it is non-demanding. It has a topography that makes the context fluctuate in orientation and scale and on which grows a robust body of a city, rather non-spectacular yet mesmerizing in the gradients of shadows. Here, I'm never overwhelmed by the scale of a built flat box. There is a sense of belonging. So, I think there is an opportunity to better collaborate with the production of industrial components so as to enrich the tools while not making them exceptional. Rather, to allow certain assemblages. Herein lies, for instance, the difference between Albini and Carlo Scarpa. Scarpa sculpted his buildings like a tailor, while Albini literally assembled. Mies assembled, Lewerentz assembled (with some parts customized); in fact, a lot of their drawings relied on standard components.

EW Do you identify as an assembler, Francesca?

FT Yes.

EH I love that. I'm now thinking about why we do things and the difficult question of how we do it. That's why I wanted to engage in the question of observation and its method. I wonder, have your methods changed over time? When do you think they were born? As a student in Mendrisio? With your diploma project, Archivio delle Acque?

FT I think that at school I made very bad projects, but during the diploma something good happened, something that still surprises me. I'm really an observer. I'm uncomfortable with romanticism and mystical attitudes, which is why I tend to keep a hard grip on rationality. I like the real – sharing stories is also real – but it's important for me not to become overly subjective. So, as a method, I always start with observation. I discuss with the people in the studio. I ask for critique. I worry about getting tricked by my mind, developing too much affection for one idea. Fondness towards people is fine, but towards ideas is irresponsible, I find – somehow hollow, in the end. We need to understand what resonates with others, sometimes in different ways than originally intended – that's true critique. This helps me to do my best. I don't like strange convolutions.

EW That feeds into the end of your lecture, where you turn to the idea of collaboration. You seem to want to make work that has a rational aspect, which enables it to be owned, emotionally and intellectually, by your clients and builders and ultimately by a wider community of people.

FT In a way, I do. I am known as being stubborn. This is because I need to understand, which is often taken as stubbornness. But when I understand an idea and I think it's fantastic, I totally jump on it. This informs my thinking about how to communicate architecture. I think it works at very different scales. I'm more like a technician. I use memories and weave stories, together with very technical reflections, so the way I communicate a work is meant to bring these subjects to life for others. Now, I don't feel I have such clarity on what architecture is as a whole. I have more clarity on specific buildings. I'm not interested in enlightening images that hold it all: I'm not interested in ideology, nor in cosmogonies of architecture as a discipline. I'm rather interested in the building. To me, a new building is a cultural act and an act of gathering; it's something that requires so much money, so much effort, so much time, it's an artefact that remains after all of us are dead. How can one think of this process as solely belonging to one time? That would be irrational, inconsistent.

EH This makes perfect sense, Francesca. It reminds me of Freddy Philipson, a wonderful architect teaching at Cambridge, and his mother, a Greek architect. She told him, 'Architects don't talk, they draw and build.' Lewerentz, for instance, hardly ever spoke about his buildings. He talked about all kinds of other things, about making and building, but not about his buildings – which doesn't make his buildings less interesting. But we live in a time where everything is a kind of mediation: everything needs to have a media overcoat to be accepted and integrated. But in your work, I have a feeling we don't need it. That's why your answer to Ellis's first question was so good, when you talked about reading.

EW To add to that, your lecture is very focused on buildings and on the relationship of buildings to cities and landscapes, things that you know endure. There's another aspect to your practice, though, which is about making objects, furniture, small household things, even bottle-openers. Can you say something about how the thinking you set out in the text informs these kinds of projects?

FT For me, it's the same body and story. Recently, I wanted to design cutlery because I can hardly find handy and dignifying spoons, which are even harder to find than forks. You can make a fork work, but spoons seem more complex. My thinking always starts from a landscape, wandering in time and geography; it involves this wonderful ambivalence of balance and unbalance. In this looseness lies a certain freedom of movement, as there is no constriction to one univocal performance. With good buildings, you can turn around, visit them again and each time live different experiences. That's what makes you want to return to a place. Even if it's a single room, you don't get bored. With objects, I feel the same: one shouldn't experience the use of an object as a burden, but find comfort and some measure of exoticism produced by the combination of the familiar and the unknown.

EH You have long been a design professor in Switzerland and Norway. How do you share this approach with your students? What teaching method do you use to transmit your own experience, and how important is teaching for you and your practice?

FT I'm committed to teaching. It's a place of hope for all that will come. In my studio in Genoa, there are quite a few former students of mine. At the core of my pedagogical approach, I ask students to learn to observe, to listen to their own observations, to resist the temptation to allow the subjective gaze to overcome reason. It makes them test what they've discovered and learn whether somebody else sees it differently. How is it that if you make a drawing of a landscape, so that we can see the place altogether, someone else can draw it differently and still get it right? Yet we also need to train our rationality; everything must function. To treat parameters well is important, numbers are our friends. As teachers, we must learn to trust and understand the lives students have lived. My students are always free to speak up. We don't give them strict indications on how to draw or model something. There is of course some direction from the team of teachers on how they can start to tell the story of the place, but it's very important that each student takes responsibility for his or her education. They need to dare to try out their own voices, they need to fall on their noses and stand up again. Stumbling is healthy, but stumbling with neither harm nor trauma, with some peacefulness, in full dignity and respect. That's how we all learn. In return, I've learned immensely from the students. That's maybe the core. They have taught me humbleness. Attentiveness. Patience. To be endlessly open.

This book would have not been possible without
the initiative of Franz König, the persistence of Iwan Strauven and Carlo Menon, the graphic narrative of Ismaël Bennani and Orfée Grandhomme, the precision of Patrick Lennon, and the support of the Flemish Government and Z33.
I am thankful for the generous criticism of Ellis Woodman and the inventive gaze of Elizabeth Hatz, for the sharp insight and encouragement of Christoph Grafe and for the sympathetic and challenging conversations with August Kraft Fossmark.
For the patience of my team, I am grateful.
I thank friends, colleagues and students for the invaluable conversations shared through the years.
The book is an open flow of thoughts, nothing final, with which some will agree and others disagree.

Francesca Torzo
Building Correctly

Authors
Francesca Torzo, Elizabeth Hatz and Ellis Woodman

Editors
Carlo Menon and Iwan Strauven

Book design
Ismaël Bennani and Orfée Grandhomme

Lithography
Laetitia Gendre

Assistant at the Q&A session
James Haynes

Copy editor
Patrick Lennon

Publishers
Accattone, Brussels
Architecture Curating Practice, Brussels
Verlag der Buchhandlung
Walther und Franz König, Köln

With the support of / Met de steun van
Flemish Government
Z33 House for Contemporary Art
Design and Architecture

Printed in Belgium by Cultura

Legal Deposit
The Royal Library of Belgium (KBR) stores archival copies and bibliographic information under legal deposit numbers D/2025/14913/02 (Accattone) and D/2023/15613/03 (Architecture Curating Practice). Data available at https://opac.kbr.be

The Deutsche Nationalbibliothek lists this publication in the Deutsche Nationalbibliografie; detailed bibliographic data are available at http://dnb.d-nb.de

© 2025 the authors, the editors, the publishers.

ISBN: 978-3-7533-0853-1

All rights reserved. No part of this publication may be reproduced or transmitted in any form or by any means, electronic or mechanical, including photocopy, recording, or any other information storage or retrieval system, without prior permission in writing from the publisher. Each author is responsible for the content of their article.

Distribution
Europe
Buchhandlung Walther König
Ehrenstraße 4,
50672 Köln (D)
Tel: +49 (0) 221 / 20 59 6 53
verlag@buchhandlung-walther-koenig.de

UK & Ireland
Cornerhouse Publications Ltd. - HOME
2 Tony Wilson Place
Manchester M15 4FN (UK)
Tel: +44 (0) 161 212 3466
publications@cornerhouse.org

Outside Europe
D.A.P. / Distributed Art Publishers, Inc.
75 Broad Street, Suite 630
New York, NY 10004 (USA)
Tel: +1 (0) 212 627 1999
orders@dapinc.com

Flanders
State of the Art

HOUSE FOR
CONTEMPORARY ART
DESIGN & ARCHITECTURE
Z33